page
128

AMERICA'S VIETNAM WAR

Also by Elizabeth Becker

When the War Was Over: The Voices of
Cambodia's Revolution and Its People

AMERICA'S
VIETNAM WAR

A Narrative History

ELIZABETH BECKER

CLARION BOOKS / NEW YORK

C.1

Clarion Books
a Houghton Mifflin Company imprint
215 Park Avenue South, New York, NY 10003
Text copyright © 1992 by Elizabeth Becker
Map by Jeanyee Wong
All rights reserved.

For information about permission to reproduce selections from this book, write to
Permissions, Houghton Mifflin Company,
2 Park Street, Boston, MA 02108.

Printed in the U.S.A.

Library of Congress Cataloging-in-Publication Data
Becker, Elizabeth
America's Vietnam War: a narrative history / by Elizabeth Becker.
p. cm.
Includes bibliographical references and indexes.
ISBN 0-395-59094-9
1. Vietnam Conflict, 1961–1975 — United States.
2. Vietnam — History — 20th century. I. Title.
DS558.B43 1992
959.704'3373—dc20   91-41144
                                                    CIP

B P 10 9 8 7 6 5 4 3 2 1

For my mother, Mavis Willenburg Becker,
and to the memory of my father,
Clayton George Becker

ACKNOWLEDGMENTS

I would like to thank my editor Henry Ferris and my agent Kathy Robbins for their dependable support. I am also grateful to my friends in Paris for helping me and my children while I wrote this book: Nadege de Noailles, Natalia Jimenez Fawcett, Jill Tarlau. And in the United States, I wish to thank my sister Susan Donovan and Ping Ferry for sending me material.

CONTENTS

PREFACE

On a rainy spring day in 1965, I walked into my high school class on contemporary world affairs and saw my teacher, Mrs. D. C. Smith, writing hurriedly across the blackboard. She ignored us as we slipped into our seats and tried to read what she had scrawled across the front and side blackboards.

When she had finished, Mrs. Smith turned around and said that American Marines had landed in Vietnam and this would change our lives. We were sixteen- and seventeen-year-old seniors at West Seattle High School, and we would graduate in a few months. We did not believe her, but Mrs. Smith altered the curriculum so that we could study Vietnam and the origins of the war and be prepared for the coming years.

The Vietnam War did change our lives, as Mrs. Smith predicted, and I have never forgotten that her first response to it was to teach us what she could about the war so we would be able to decide for ourselves what we thought of it. In the same spirit, I have written this history of the war. I have based it on the Pentagon Papers, supplemented with first-person accounts, other official documents, and the wealth of scholarly studies published over the past decade. Above all, I have tried to write a narrative history that explains the Vietnam War without being encyclopedic.

The Vietnam War began as a fight against French colonialism. Later, after the French were defeated, the United States joined in battle to prevent the Vietnamese communists from winning the whole country. Indeed, the wars in Vietnam lasted so long that they came to represent the ideological conflicts of the twentieth century, especially the Cold War, which pitted the democratic, free-market nations against the communist world. What is remarkable is that even though the United States won the Cold War it lost in Vietnam. I try to explain this paradox and to put the American effort in the context of its times.

Vietnam was not like the Second World War or the recent Persian Gulf war. How the United States chose to make Vietnam the site of the most costly battle against communism is a tragic tale of ideological competition driven out of all proportion. It is also the story of leaders too proud to say they have made a mistake. William Shakespeare would have understood Vietnam better than the father of communism, Karl Marx.

Finally, Vietnam has become more than a war in the popular imagination. In movies, gunmen shoot their way back into communist Vietnam to free missing American soldiers and save America's honor. In novels, Vietnam veterans are the symbol of lost American innocence twisted into madness. Underneath those stories and stereotypes is the real war that should speak for itself. This is what I have tried to do in *America's Vietnam War*.

AMERICA'S VIETNAM WAR

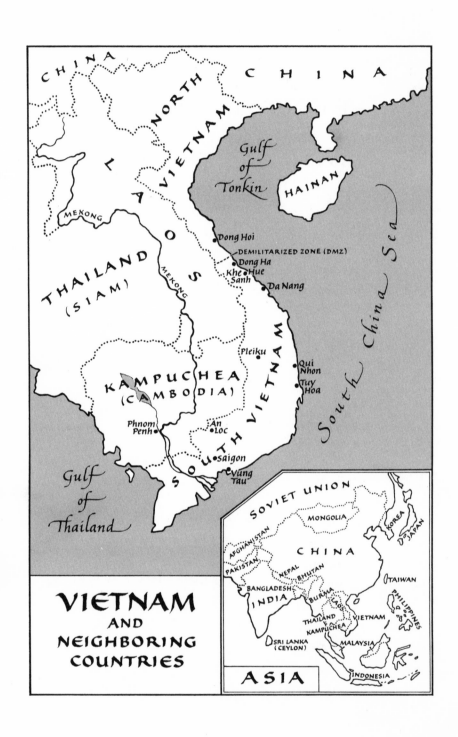

VIETNAM
AND
NEIGHBORING
COUNTRIES

1

THE COUNTRY VIETNAM

Although we have been at times strong,
at times weak,
we have at no time lacked heroes.
*Vietnamese saying from
the fifteenth century*

THE HISTORY OF Vietnam is a two-thousand-year-long saga filled with war, conquest, and political intrigue. The recent American war in Vietnam was neither the longest, nor the bloodiest. As is true of many of the world's older civilizations, Vietnam's conflicts have been fed by its geography.

Vietnam sits on the southeastern edge of the great Asian continent. Its southern tip is land's end of the peninsula known as Indochina. Vietnam's long eastern border is the South China Sea; its short southern boundary is the Gulf of Siam. To the west are Cambodia and Laos, and beyond them the rest of Southeast Asia. But to the north is China, an immense, rich, and powerful country that has cast a long shadow over Vietnamese history.

Vietnam, or Nam Viet, was a small, young civilization

at the dawn of the Christian era, when the Chinese invaded and made it part of their empire. Around A.D. 10, when the Chinese started to colonize the country, its area was only one-third the size it is today. The people lived in the Red River Valley region of northernmost Vietnam. Small peaked mountains shelter this valley and give it a haunting beauty. Mists rise from the river and blanket the fields where the people have cultivated rice for centuries. Here the Chinese brought their own culture and forced the Vietnamese people to learn their language, accept their domination, and transform their society into a copy of China's.

From the beginning the Vietnamese rebelled at the notion of becoming Chinese. In the year 40, two noble-women known as the Trung sisters led a rebellion that failed but has not been forgotten. Even today the Vietnamese celebrate the anniversary of their attempt to throw out the Chinese. Other revolts followed. In the third century and again in the fifth, seventh, and eighth centuries, other Vietnamese leaders tried to push out the Chinese. These heroes and heroines kept alive the hope and ambition to free their country from foreign domination.

Finally, in 939, the Vietnamese defeated the Chinese and won their independence. Nearly a thousand years of Chinese rule was over. But China's influence was not so easily erased. After centuries of domination, nearly every aspect of Vietnamese life was profoundly marked by China. Vietnam's royal court strongly resembled the court of the Chinese. The country was governed by the scholarly men known as mandarins, very much in the Chinese tradition. The elite Vietnamese practiced Confucianism, the religious philosophy founded in China. And although many Vietnamese also followed the Buddhist faith, it was the Chinese form of Buddhism, rather than that followed in the rest of Southeast Asia. Most striking, the official language remained Chinese.

Fortunately, underneath this rich, nearly suffocating layer of Chinese culture, Vietnamese civilization was alive, especially in the countryside. In the villages off the main roads, the common people never had become entirely "Chinese." Hidden behind thick screens of bamboo, the farming hamlets had preserved the rural Vietnamese culture. Their life was governed as much by the monsoon rains that soaked the rice paddies and filled the rivers as by the Chinese. The Vietnamese language and folkways were preserved by these hard-working farmers and fishermen.

Freed from the Chinese, the Vietnamese sought to establish themselves as an important power. They wanted to enlarge their country, to break out of the Red River Valley, with its encircling and limiting mountains. They could not move north, for that territory was under the rule of China. They had to go south, where the countries were smaller and weaker and where the land was fertile. They declared war on their southern neighbors, the Chams and the Cambodians. Over the next several centuries the Vietnamese continued to push south, taking more territory and increasing their wealth.

The Vietnamese called this expansion their March South, or Nam-Tien. They considered it part of their historic destiny, much as the American pioneers thought of their westward movement toward the Pacific Ocean. The Vietnamese conquered the south by defeating armies and destroying other civilizations, by negotiating treaties and grabbing land.

In the fifteenth century the Vietnamese were briefly

stopped by the Chinese reconquest of their country. But once again the Vietnamese did not lack heroes. A man named Le Loi enlisted the people in a guerrilla war against the Chinese and succeeded in driving them out. With his power and stature, Le Loi became the ruler of Vietnam and began the great Le dynasty.

In 1471 the Vietnamese defeated the Chams, their immediate neighbors to the south, and took over all of present-day central Vietnam. They were ready to mount their final campaign to win the rich, fertile Mekong River delta from the Cambodians, thereby controlling all the land from the Red River to the Gulf of Siam.

Some 150 years later, in 1765, the Vietnamese completed their March South, a triumph of determination as well as military prowess. Vietnam had become a country of warriors who fought well on land and sea. The Vietnamese now ruled a country larger than the western U.S. state of New Mexico.

After the March South, Vietnamese said their country looked like one of the narrow poles peasants carry on their shoulders; the two fan-shaped delta regions, the Red River in the north and the Mekong River in the south, were the "baskets" at the ends of the pole, which consisted of a thin strip of hills and mountains.

Vietnam was now a wealthy country. The tropical Mekong delta was ideal for growing rice, the staple of the Vietnamese diet, and an abundance of fruit and vegetables. The waters of the south were brimming with fish to add to the national diet. The country's coastline was a thousand miles long. Vietnam had become a great maritime state in the region, and its sailors were among Asia's most accomplished.

Vietnam was a nation of "water, rice and men," as a prominent Vietnamese writer noted: water for travel, fishing, and irrigation; rice for nourishment; and the determined character of the people to propel Vietnam to greatness.

By the end of the eighteenth century, about the time the United States won its independence from England, Vietnam was one of the rising powers of mainland Southeast Asia. Its chief rival was Siam, the country known today as Thailand.

The Vietnamese were convinced that they were truly exceptional people. They saw themselves as courageous freedom fighters who had thrown out the Chinese colonizers after almost a thousand years of humiliation. They saw themselves as brilliant military conquerors whose March South had fulfilled their country's destiny.

However, the Chams and Cambodians who had been defeated thought the Vietnamese were brutal expansionists and extremely arrogant people. They had treated the Chams and Cambodians as if they were inferior or barbarians and had shown little respect for their different but rich cultures. As a result, and perhaps because of the influence of the Chinese notion of superiority, the Vietnamese developed what one historian has called "a proud, almost haughty tradition."

The country's huge expansion was not without cost. In the eighteenth century the Vietnamese began fighting among themselves about who should rule the new territory. A rival dynasty laid claim to the south and called itself the Nguyen dynasty. The Le dynasty that ruled northern Vietnam did not want to share power and began a war to unify the country, but it was defeated in 1802. The Nguyen dynasty won the war with crucial aid from French missionaries and French mercenaries — soldiers for hire.

The Nguyen dynasty moved the country's capital from Hanoi to Hue in central Vietnam and built a grand new court. Among those attending the new emperor were scholars and bureaucrats who had served the defeated Le dynasty. One such mandarin was Nguyen Du. He was a poet as well as a statesman, and he was heartbroken that this new dynasty of "upstarts" had overthrown the Le dynasty. Unable to deny his feelings, Nguyen Du wrote an epic poem, almost a novel, that became known as *The Tale of Khieu*. The poem, a love story, is considered an allegory, for it speaks symbolically of the poet's sadness that he must serve the Nguyen dynasty, which destroyed the dynasty he respected and loved. *The Tale of Khieu*, a literary masterpiece, became Vietnam's best-loved story.

Khieu is a young noblewoman who is forced to betray her family, her loyalties, and her beliefs. First she is tricked into becoming a prostitute, but she frees herself by running away with a married man, whose angry wife devises a scheme for getting rid of Khieu. Then the heroine falls in love with another man, a courageous rebel who is thought to be one of the greatest characters in Vietnamese literature. A man with "a tiger's beard, a jaw like a swallow's beak, brows thick as silkworms," the rebel is eventually killed when he refuses to give up his independence to join the royal court. In the poem the rebel explains why:

> *My own two hands have built this realm of mine.*
> *I roam the streams and seas just as I wish.*
> *If I submit, surrender all my power,*
> *and show my shamed, confounded face at court,*
> *what will become of me among them all?*

Every Vietnamese could understand his sentiments. Over the next century *The Tale of Khieu* became a metaphor for any number of situations in which Vietnamese saw themselves, like Khieu, as victims of a perverse fate. During the French colonial period, the French war, and finally the American war, Vietnamese could be found reciting *The Tale of Khieu* because it resounded with the melancholy, hope, despair, and wisdom of a proud people whose aspirations are dashed by fate.

The French Conquest

European travelers and traders had begun visiting Southeast Asia around 1511, when the Portuguese first arrived. But even though the Nguyen dynasty used French help in 1802 to defeat the Le dynasty, successive Vietnamese emperors were wary of the French and tried to expel the "barbarians from the West." They did not want the French to make inroads into their society, to change their culture, or, worse, to take control of their country. After 1825 Emperor Minh Mang refused to allow further trade with the French, and beginning in 1834 he punished any Vietnamese who converted to the Roman Catholic faith practiced by the French missionaries.

But France was not so easily dissuaded. The European powers wanted colonies; France and England had become rivals for control in the Far East, both wanting the wealth, power, and prestige of an empire. And with their modern weapons and armies, these European powers were able to defeat the Asian countries that fought to keep them out.

The first French attack came when the Vietnamese put

to death two Catholic missionaries in 1851–52. Then in 1859 the French captured Saigon in the south, and three years later they took over three Vietnamese provinces. The French forced the Vietnamese to allow French missionaries to return and continue their efforts to convert the people to Catholicism. With such steps, over the next twenty years the French forced the Vietnamese to give up ever more land and authority. Finally, in 1883 the French attacked the capital, Hue, in preparation for taking control of the entire country, which they did in 1886, making Vietnam a French protectorate.

The proud Vietnamese were once again under foreign rule. The struggle to free themselves from France would be just as difficult, if not nearly as long, as the earlier battle to free themselves from Chinese rule.

French Colonialism and Vietnamese Nationalism

Why is the roof of their [the Western] universe the broad
* land and skies,*
While we cower and confine ourselves to a cranny in our
* house?*
Why can they jump straight, leap far,
While we shrink back and cling to each other?
Why do they rule the world,
While we bow our heads as slaves?
Take up a mirror, look at yourself.
Where on that face is there something to brag about? . . .
We have eyes, but they seem to be blind.
Who will bring the lamp to light the path?

This poem, written by a Vietnamese patriot in 1905, illustrates the strong, tough nationalist feelings that grew out of shame and then anger over French colonial rule. This is the nationalism that inspired the Vietnamese who eventually fought in the Indochina wars. For many Vietnamese, America's Vietnam War was a continuation of the bitter struggle against French colonialism.

The French ruled the country by first dividing it. North and central Vietnam were ruled as separate protectorates, called Tonkin and Annam respectively. South Vietnam was ruled as a full-fledged colony named Cochin China. The country of Vietnam no longer existed. The people were known by the French as Tonkinese, Annamites, and Cochin Chinese rather than Vietnamese. Tonkin, Annam, and Cochin China were part of the Indochinese Union, which included neighboring Cambodia and Laos. The Indochinese Union was one of France's most cherished colonial possessions.

The French ruled all aspects of Vietnam's life — cultural, economic, political, and military. They demanded that the Vietnamese conform to their culture, which the French considered vastly superior to Vietnam's. The Vietnamese had to learn the French language and copy French behavior and dress if they wanted to succeed in their own country. The French built up Saigon as their administrative capital, and it became known as the Paris of the Orient, with café society, French police, and grand boulevards. Within this society the Vietnamese were swiftly demoted to second-class citizens.

The first reactions to this loss of status were a combination of shock, despair, and anger. One of the first Vietnamese dissidents said, "They [the French] all show dislike and disdain for the Vietnamese, considering them savages, comparing them with pigs and cows, unwilling to let them become equals."

The mandarins, the small elite of scholars, were among the first to rebel and speak out against French rule. They were haunted by the fear of *mat nouc*, of losing their national cultural identity — literally losing their country. The French expected the Vietnamese elite to become "assimilated," to become Oriental imitations of themselves. At the turn of the century, the French abolished the system of mandarins.

Soon other Vietnamese classes were also threatened by the effects of French colonial rule. Within fifty years of its occupation by France, the country had become a classic colony. The French ran Vietnam's commercial life, levying taxes, imposing import and export duties, and introducing their own systems of land holding and marketing goods. The French owners profited from all forms of production, including the harvest of the fields, farms, and orchards; ore from the mines; handicrafts; and simple labor. The French controlled all aspects of the rice trade, rubber production, and mining. France introduced rubber and coffee plantations to the Indochinese countries and used Vietnamese coolie labor to work them.

Little of the money raised from taxes or earned in business was reinvested in Vietnam. Most of the profits were sent back to the French government or kept by the businessmen. The colonial authorities did construct roads, build railroads, and invest in other public works, but not on the scale the Vietnamese considered commensurate with the profits that were being taken out of the country. Equally discouraging was the French policy toward industrialization. They imported their own manufactured goods and expected the Vietnamese to purchase them rather than develop their own industries.

Unwittingly the French, simply by introducing French ideas in their schools, encouraged the Vietnamese students to criticize these policies. The French taught the philosophies of writers such as Jean-Jacques Rousseau, who emphasized freedom and compassion. Students influenced by Rousseau and other Western philosophers helped turn the country's anticolonial impulses into modern visions of freedom, democracy, and, eventually, revolution.

The slogan "Don't Pay Taxes to the French," first used in 1908, was followed by other protests against abysmally low wages and prohibitions against native newspapers and freedom of expression. With each nonviolent protest the Vietnamese realized that they wanted desperately to get rid of the French and rule themselves again.

Some Vietnamese thought ahead, imagining what their country would be like after independence. They did not want to return to the old style of royal government with its corrupt, arbitrary officials, its elitism and authoritarianism. They wanted to become a modern democracy. And they translated these ideas into action. Vietnamese workers called strikes against their French employers. Nationalists organized political parties quietly and secretly to avoid arrest by the French police. Vietnamese were not allowed to have their own parties, much less challenge their rulers.

While the Vietnamese were organizing their opposition to French colonialism, the world was changing. When the First World War broke out in Europe in 1914, the French government forced 100,000 Vietnamese to serve in their army and fight in that faraway war. Incensed, one Vietnamese patriot chastised his countrymen for fighting beside the French: "We still kneel down, bow our heads, kow-tow to the French like gods, revere them like saints, slaves to them all our lives. . . . Will we continue to stand around and stomach this shame forever?"

During the Great Depression, which began in 1929, colonies like Vietnam suffered doubly. Profits and taxes from the colonies went to help the mother country, and the Vietnamese were left with little. More and more Vietnamese, deciding they could no longer meekly accept French rule, began to resist nonviolently. As anticolonial agitation grew, the French took a severe, stubborn stance against granting any new freedoms to their colony. In response the Vietnamese changed the character of their resistance to violent defiance.

This transformation was aided by the rebels of Vietnam. One was Ho Chi Minh. Born into a mandarin family in central Vietnam in 1890, he had witnessed his father and early teachers agonizing over whether to resist French rule or to collaborate and avoid conflict, hoping for eventual independence. When he was a teenager, Ho Chi Minh abandoned his program of French studies and left Vietnam to search for a program for freeing his country from the French and providing it with a modern form of government. His wanderings took him to the United States and to France, where he settled. In 1920 the thirty-year-old Ho became a founding member of the French Communist party. In those days the communist program seemed modern and open to ideas; most important for Ho Chi Minh, it was the one party in France opposed to colonial rule in Indochina. Communists were openly campaigning against colonial empires as unjust and unfair, the exploitation of one people by another. Ho Chi Minh decided that this new form of government was the best for Vietnam. It was a decision that would separate Vietnam from most of the other Asian nations struggling to free themselves from European rule and eventually lead it on a collision course with the United States.

The War Against the French

In the 1920s and 1930s, between the First and the Second World War, Vietnamese nationalists opposed to French colonialism sampled every new Western and Oriental philosophy they could find. If the French colonial authorities forbade a book about democracy written in French or Vietnamese, they would read it in a Japanese translation. Ultimately, the most organized and powerful Vietnamese dissidents chose communism as the ideology that could bring them independence and a modern government. In 1930 these Vietnamese formed the Indochinese Communist party. Their top leader, Ho Chi Minh, was trained by the Soviet communists, who also directed the organization of the party. Communism offered these Asians a powerful form of organization, opposition to foreign colonialism, and, like other political philosophies of the twentieth century, promises of economic prosperity and equality as well as democracy — promises the communist system failed to keep over the next decades.

The Second World War broke out in 1939, and in the

summer of 1940 the German army occupied France. This had a powerful effect on Vietnam. The Japanese were allies of Nazi Germany in the Fascist Axis, and Germany forced France to allow the Japanese to establish bases in all the Indochinese colonies, in Cambodia and Laos as well as Vietnam. The Japanese left the French colonial bureaucracy in place to govern Vietnam while they swept through Southeast Asia expanding their empire. The Japanese were a new enemy in Vietnam. They committed atrocities throughout the region, executing those they considered their enemies and taking away rice and other food, often creating near-famine conditions.

The Vietnamese communists, led by Ho Chi Minh, created the Viet Minh, an organization that included all Vietnamese anticolonialists who were fighting the French and the Japanese. Toward the end of the war the Japanese took full control of Vietnam from the French, and Ho Chi Minh worked briefly with the Americans against the Japanese. From the spring through the summer of 1945, the Viet Minh helped American intelligence officers devise strategies against the Japanese. Then the Americans dropped atomic bombs on Hiroshima and Nagasaki, forcing the Japanese to surrender. The brief alliance between the Viet Minh and the United States came to a close.

At the end of the war, on August 25, 1945, Ho Chi Minh declared Vietnam an independent country. He and his small Viet Minh army marched into Hanoi the next day, and on September 2 he read their proclamation of independence. It began, "All men are created equal. They are endowed by their Creator with certain inalienable rights. Among these are Life, Liberty and the pursuit of Happiness." He had borrowed the preamble of America's Declaration of Independence for Vietnam.

The Vietnamese emperor, Bao Dai, abdicated in favor of this new independent government. Then the Allied troops, under British and Nationalist Chinese command, began arriving in Vietnam to take the Japanese surrender and ensure an orderly transition to a new government. For the Allies, the question was, *what* government?

The answer to that question was the first Indochina War, between the French, who wanted to keep Vietnam under their control, and the Vietnamese communists, who believed they had won their country's independence.

The First Indochina War

While other European nations were beginning the painful process of freeing their colonies and letting them become modern, independent nations, France wanted to reconquer Indochina. During the Second World War, President Franklin D. Roosevelt had said he wanted all colonies freed, and Ho Chi Minh expected America's political support for his declaration of independence. But after Roosevelt's death the new president, Harry S. Truman, decided not to block the French from taking back their Indochinese colonies.

From 1945 through 1946 the French and the Viet Minh tried to work out a compromise, but the French wanted to make the south of Vietnam a separate country and to disarm all the Vietnamese militia. They did not want to reunify Vietnam or even grant it partial independence. The two sides attended conferences without results, and finally war broke out between them. In November 1946 French ships shelled the northern Vietnamese harbor city of Haiphong, killing 6,000 civilians.

From the beginning, both sides in this war expected support from the United States. In 1946 the United States was the most powerful nation in the world, the only country with the atomic bomb and a strong postwar economy. At first the American government practiced what has been called "active neutrality" in favor of France because it was less interested in the far-off nation of Vietnam than in its old and vulnerable European ally.

The Cold War between the United States and the Soviet Union was under way. Under the dictator Joseph Stalin, the Soviet Union had taken control of most of the states of eastern Europe and made them part of the Soviet bloc. President Truman wanted to contain the spread of communism and stop the Soviet Union from taking over other European nations. American experts feared that France was the most likely Western European nation to elect a communist government. So, hoping that France would continue working with the other European democracies in a common defense against Soviet communism, the United States did not protest France's war to retake its colonies.

Ho Chi Minh, remembering President Roosevelt's declarations in favor of independence for colonies, asked the United States to recognize his Viet Minh government. The United States simply refused to answer his appeals. Instead, under the Marshall Plan, which the United States created to help rebuild western Europe after the Second World War, the Americans gave France aid to repair war damages, allowing the French to use money from its own treasury to fight the war in Vietnam.

America continued to worry more about France than

Vietnam as the Cold War grew more serious. In 1948 the Soviet Union took over Czechoslovakia and announced the blockade of Berlin. The United States and the western European nations, including France, formed the North Atlantic Treaty Organization (NATO) to create a common defense. At the same time France was demanding American financial support for its war to control Vietnam. The American secretary of state, Dean Acheson, said the French were "blackmailing" the U.S. government into accepting this outdated colonial war, by threatening not to provide troops for NATO.

But events in Asia made the United States think differently about Vietnam. In October 1949 the Chinese communists under Mao Tse-tung won the civil war and became the leaders of China, and in 1950 communist North Korea invaded noncommunist South Korea. Suddenly communism seemed to be making far greater headway in Asia than in Europe, and American policy makers began worrying about the communist threat in the Far East. The war in Vietnam no longer looked like a French attempt at colonial reconquest but like a communist plan instigated by the Soviet Union to conquer more of Asia. The Americans viewed Ho Chi Minh as an agent of the Soviet Union who wanted to put Vietnam into the Soviet communist bloc. Vietnam became part of the new ideological battle between communism and noncommunism. In truth, the Indochina War was both an attempt by Vietnam to become independent of a colonial power and an attempt to make it part of the communist world.

American policy makers now supported the French, hoping to save Vietnam, and perhaps other Southeast Asian nations, from Soviet communism. The United States was willing to support France directly in exchange for a promise to grant the Vietnamese some form of independence. But the French were not fighting an anticommunist crusade; they were fighting to hold on to their colonies, and they refused to make such a promise.

Ho Chi Minh was not acting as a dupe of Soviet communism. At this stage, the Soviet Union was not giving him any money and was not in charge of his army or his fledgling government. Ho Chi Minh was in charge, and his reputation as a nationalist was growing because he was standing up to the French. He stressed the war for independence and downplayed his belief in communism, although he had ruthlessly eliminated many noncommunist challengers to the Viet Minh. The Vietnamese people increasingly accepted Ho Chi Minh's view of the war as a struggle against French colonialism.

The Truman administration gave the French $133 million in direct aid, including weapons, ammunition, ships, trucks, and airplanes. The French accepted the aid but still refused to promise greater political freedom for the Vietnamese. From 1950 onward, the United States gave nonmilitary aid to French-held Vietnam: medicine, food, and clothing for the people, seeds and fertilizer for their fields.

But the French were losing the war. By the early 1950s the Viet Minh controlled two-thirds of the countryside. Their army was led by a former schoolteacher named General Vo Nguyen Giap, who was gaining a national reputation for his victories. The Americans convinced the French to create a Vietnamese army to fight alongside them to give the appearance of Vietnamese support for the French, but few Vietnamese wanted to help the French reassert colonial control.

In 1952, as the French military position worsened, the Americans came to their rescue with another $150 million in aid. That year General Dwight D. Eisenhower, a hero of the Second World War, was elected president of the United States, but he made no changes in American policy toward Vietnam.

Eisenhower did pressure the French to plan larger, more decisive military operations to defeat the Viet Minh. They settled on a plan for a French-held outpost in northwestern Vietnam called Dien Bien Phu, and the United States gave France another $385 million in aid. In November 1953 the stage was set for the last great battle of the war, the siege of Dien Bien Phu.

The French built up the garrison at Dien Bien Phu to bait the Viet Minh into fighting a classical battle, which the French believed they could win with their superior modern firepower. Instead of falling into this trap, General Giap devised a simple strategy. His army avoided the roads that would have led to direct combat with the French, traveling instead over rugged mountains and terrain the French had considered impassable. The Viet Minh surprised the French by capturing the high ground around Dien Bien Phu and shelling the outpost for fifty-six days until the French were forced to surrender. The Viet Minh victory came on May 7, 1954, just one day before an East-West conference in Geneva was to begin negotiating a settlement of the Indochina War.

Dien Bien Phu was "one of the truly decisive battles of the twentieth century," wrote Bernard B. Fall, a leading historian of Vietnam at war. After that siege it was clear that the French could no longer achieve "whatever it had sought to gain in fighting the war," and Ho Chi Minh's army was seen as the force that had freed Vietnam of the French colonialists. Dien Bien Phu became a symbol of the Viet Minh's refusal to cede the advantage to the enemy, no matter what hardships or how many lives it cost to achieve military control.

The French loss was great. Some 50,000 French soldiers had been killed, 2,000 in the battle of Dien Bien Phu alone. Every three years during the war an entire class of St. Cyr, the French military academy, died on the battlefield. Some 25,000 soldiers were missing at war's end, most of whom were later declared dead, and some 100,000 had been wounded. The French had spent more money on the Indochina War than they had received from the United States under the Marshall Plan.

This was more than enough for the French people. Weakened by the war, they chose a new leader, Pierre Mendès-France, who promised to end French involvement in Indochina in July of that year.

At the Geneva Conference in May 1954 the French agreed to leave Vietnam. A partial political solution to the war, including a cease-fire, was agreed upon. In attendance were delegations from France, Great Britain, the United States, China, the Soviet Union, and the three countries of Indochina. The United States had refused to recognize communist China, so the American representative was forbidden to talk to the Chinese. The Viet Minh refused to talk to the French. The final compromise was achieved in discussions between French prime minister Mendès-France and Chinese foreign minister Chou En-lai.

France and the Viet Minh agreed that Vietnam would be divided temporarily, for two years, at the seventeenth parallel until national elections were held to choose a leader of the whole country. The Viet Minh agreed to withdraw its troops from the south while the French left the north. There was to be a cease-fire in Vietnam, Cambodia, and Laos.

However, the United States did not sign the Geneva accords, nor did the Vietnamese in the south. The Viet Minh were unhappy with the accords; they privately felt betrayed by the Chinese communists, who brokered the compromise that forced them to give up half the country. Both the Chinese and Soviet communists had pressured the Viet Minh to accept this compromise to avoid an open confrontation with the United States.

By the time the war ended, it had become an American war. The United States had begun paying nearly 80 percent of the French war costs, totaling some $2.6 billion. And the Americans had redefined what they thought was at stake in Vietnam. During the siege of Dien Bien Phu, President Eisenhower made the comparison between a communist victory in Vietnam and a game of dominoes. He said that if Indochina was lost to the communists, other Southeast Asian nations would fall like a "row of dominoes" to communism.

From that day the "domino theory" became a major part of America's political vision. It became shorthand for America's fear that communism would spread throughout Asia if the United States did not stop it in Vietnam. The United States saw that small country as the front line of its war against communism. Successive American administrations grew more fearful, believing that if the Vietnamese communists won, then the Soviet Union or communist China would fight to take over not only Southeast Asia but the United States itself.

2

WAR OR PEACE

AFTER THE Geneva Conference, as the French army prepared to leave Vietnam, the citizens of the south were worried. Saigon was still administered by members of the French colonial bureaucracy and protected by French soldiers. The southerners feared that chaos would replace the French colonizers and that the small South Vietnamese army would be unable to keep the peace.

Then Bao Dai, the former emperor, who was appointed chief of state under the French, asked Ngo Dinh Diem to come to Saigon from Paris and head a new government, one that would transform the south into a modern state and calm the people during this unsettling, nervous time. Diem was a cultured man and a patriot who had earned a reputation for integrity among his countrymen. The Americans considered him a strong anticommunist. He had no experience as a leader, but as the French historian Paul Mus wrote in 1948, "Only one man could ever hope to challenge Ho Chi Minh for leadership — Ngo Dinh Diem. Because he alone has the same reputation for virtue and austerity as Ho. Vietnamese will only follow a man who is known to be virtuous and who leads an austere life."

But the differences between Ho Chi Minh and Diem were greater than their similarities. The son of a prosperous elite family from Hue, Diem had been raised as a Catholic, an outsider in Confucian and Buddhist Vietnam. He had refused to take a position in the French colonial system, but he had also refused to fight the French. He wanted to improve the life of peasants, but he had no practical notion of how to accomplish this goal, and he feared that the communists had greater appeal. He wrote in one pamphlet, "The Communists will defeat us not by virtue of their strength but because of our weakness." There was more than a hint of imperiousness in Diem's nature. But American leaders believed nonetheless that he could become the father of democracy in South Vietnam.

Few Vietnamese went to the airport to greet Diem when he flew into Saigon in July 1954 to become the south's prime minister. On that day he promised that his new government would offer "complete independence . . . complete democracy and direct participation of the people in affairs of State." He had no idea how he would accomplish any of these goals. Bao Dai had given him power to run the government, but none of the south's political groups supported him, and he did not have the backing of the army. Several rival political groups had their own private armies, which also threatened Diem's power.

Diem's main foreign support came from several influential American Catholics, including the young U.S. Senator John F. Kennedy. Diem had also become friends with Supreme Court Justice William O. Douglas and Senator Mike Mansfield during a sojourn in the United States. But the fifty-three-year-old Diem had to prove himself in South Vietnam before his American friends could help him. The United States had agreed to underwrite the new state of South Vietnam, but the Americans had not decided who was the best man to head the government.

Diem's task was enormous. Saigonese generally remembered two things about him: how he had honorably quit the prestigious job of minister of the interior at the court of Hue in 1932 to protest French colonial rule, and his less attractive behavior as a *tram chan,* someone who "hid under a blanket," to avoid fighting in the French war. Both the regular army and the private armies expected Diem to fail quickly in the face of physical danger from rivals, clearing the way for them to rule South Vietnam.

Diem's mission was even more complicated. With Ho Chi Minh speaking out against the division of Vietnam, Diem was in the position of trying to put together a government based on a divided country, even though the Geneva Accords called for unification following the 1956 general elections.

Indeed, Diem was nearly paralyzed by the situation, and during the first months he barely left his office. Saigon was waiting him out. The sophisticated river port was filled with businessmen and politicians as well as generals who preferred conspiracies to democracy. The military men were discussing how to overthrow Diem. Saigon's passive bureaucrats continued their old custom of obstructing government business and bringing the administration to a standstill. Diem had to find the levers of control in a city that preferred anarchy. He had to gain power over the army and find a political base that would support him, thereby proving to the Americans that he could rule.

In the midst of this crisis, Diem heard news that drove him nearly to despair. The communists were preparing to take power in the north, and the French army was evacuating, abandoning the enclaves of Vietnamese Catholics there. In response to this situation, the United States Central Intelligence Agency (CIA) had Major Lucien Conein lead a secret, illegal sabotage mission to the north to instigate a mass exodus of Vietnamese Catholics to the south. Conein's team disrupted public transportation, blew up fuel dumps, and spread rumors to frighten the people. The mission was successful, perhaps because the Catholics wanted to leave anyway. According to a secret American report written at the time, the CIA team wanted to frighten the Catholics and made up "leaflets signed by the Vietminh instructing [northerners] on how to behave for the Vietminh takeover of the Hanoi region ... including items about property, money reform, and a three-day holiday of workers upon takeover. The day following the distribution of these leaflets refugee registration tripled."

Some 860,000 Vietnamese were frightened enough by the propaganda to flee the north. Diem asked the United States for ships and aircraft to transport the refugees to the south and for money to house and feed them once they arrived. The Catholics, who made up the majority of the refugees, were well organized; often an entire village traveled together, led by their priest. Once they settled in the south, these Catholics became Diem's staunchest supporters.

Around the same time Diem received key support from another American officer living in Saigon, air force colonel Edward G. Lansdale, who was on assignment with the CIA. Lansdale was a handsome, sincere, but superficial man who had made his name successfully fighting insurgents in the Philippines. To Lansdale, Vietnam was just another Southeast Asian nation that needed his expertise to defeat a group of communist insurgents in the jungles. He believed that the methods he had used in the Philippines would work equally well in Vietnam. His confidence was contagious. Diem accepted Lansdale's advice and his CIA money. He needed both.

By Diem's fourth month in office in 1954, the South Vietnamese army was preparing a coup d'état to overthrow him, and several private armies were plotting a revolt. Lansdale told Diem to buy off his enemies. The U.S. ambassador in Saigon quietly requested the money from Washington. Official records show that "the U.S. secretly furnished Diem with funds" for one general in particular, General Trinh Minh The, who headed a private army for the Cao Dai religious sect. Altogether, Lansdale channeled as much as $10 million to Diem to buy the loyalty of the various private armies.

The Americans used a different tactic with South Vietnamese army officers who were plotting a coup. The U.S. government made a public statement that American military aid to South Vietnam would continue only if the army officers supported Ngo Dinh Diem's government. Two days later the general planning the coup flew to Paris.

Diem should have been safe; he now had the army under his control and the private armies quieted with bribes. To demonstrate this newfound stability, in January 1955 the government staged a public rally during which former dissident General The, with millions of dollars in secret CIA funds in his pocket, crossed over to Diem's side. This ceremony was meant to underline Diem's appeal to and control over all the warring factions of the south.

But the south was not so easily tamed. Two months later, at the beginning of the withering hot season, the private armies, along with several small religious sects, staged a public protest against Diem's dominance and demanded a "United Front of Nationalist Forces." Joining the protest was General The, still rich but no longer an ally of Diem's.

The loud, threatening protest showed that Diem's hold on power was as fragile as the Americans had first feared. A personal emissary from President Eisenhower concluded in a report to Washington that Diem "does not have the capacity to achieve the necessary unity of purpose and action from his people which is essential to prevent this country from falling under communist control."

The emissary was General J. Lawton Collins, who also said of Diem, "His lack of practical political sense, his inability to compromise, his inherent incapacity to get along with other able men and his tendency to be suspicious of the motives of anyone who disagrees with him, make him practically incapable of holding this government together."

Other U.S. intelligence reports agreed with Collins's appraisal; he and other American officials in Saigon sent to Washington the names of potential replacements for Diem. The Americans were beginning to act like the French before them, believing they had the right to decide who should rule Vietnam.

Diem knew that the United States was looking for a replacement for him, and he rose to the challenge. On the strong advice of his brother, Ngo Dinh Nhu, Diem ordered one of the most notorious private armies to end its rebellion against his regime. When the private army refused, Nhu told his brother, "Fight back." In April 1955 Diem ordered the South Vietnamese army to fight this rebellious private army, and the streets of Saigon were turned into bloody battle-fields. Cannon shells and bullets tore into homes and gardens, shops and offices. Nearly 500 civilians were killed in the street fighting, and another 20,000 were made homeless.

Diem won, and the leader of the private army fled to Paris. The other private forces gave up their resistance to Diem, but not before some 2,000 rallied to the side of the communists. Diem had achieved power finally, not by defeating the communists but by fighting or alienating his fellow noncommunists in the south.

Saigon

The Americans living in South Vietnam in the mid-1950s must have found this byzantine society quite confusing, with various Vietnamese religious sects, including one that worshiped the French poet Victor Hugo, Jesus Christ, and Buddha. The corruption of Saigon was so interwoven with politics it was impossible to separate drug trafficking from presidential politics. All important meetings were held behind closed doors, in alleyways or cellars or private mansions. Three languages — Vietnamese, Chinese, and

French — were used for business, and English soon became the fourth. Always there were communists hiding, waiting to take over, by force if necessary.

Fortunately Saigon and the south were open to anyone with eyes and ears. It had always been a city of gossip and intrigue. Money could buy information, and patience could lead one to as much truth as one wanted to learn.

Many American officials understood and reported the weaknesses of the Saigon regime in confidential cables sent back to Washington. But they refused to admit those weaknesses would lead to defeat, and in public they were always optimistic, giving the whole American enterprise an air of misguided innocence. But British writer Graham Greene published a novel in 1955 called *The Quiet American* that revealed all the intricacies of the south, and all the problems America was having in finding a candidate to head a democracy that did not yet exist. Greene even created a character very much like Lansdale, who gave secret CIA money to a General The.

Greene's CIA character was as well-meaning and as dangerous as the real Lansdale. Another character in the novel said of the CIA man, "I never knew a man who had better motives for all the trouble he caused." In the novel the CIA agent gave General The money to create a democratic alternative to the communists. Instead, the general hid bombs on bicycles, which blew up dozens of innocent people one morning on a busy Saigon square. Greene described that scene: "A woman sat on the ground with what was left of her baby in her lap; with a kind of modesty she had covered it with her straw peasant hat. She sat still and silent."

The scene was based on a real incident, and most of the

novel was based on Greene's observations while visiting Saigon. His ability to capture the truth was proved over a decade later with the publication of the secret U.S. government documents known as the Pentagon Papers, which told the history of American involvement in Vietnam.

In fact, *The Quiet American* was considered too close to reality from the moment of its publication and was banned by the government in Saigon. In literary circles it has become known as the eternal Vietnam novel.

Diem's victory over the rebellious private army stunned the U.S. government. Literally overnight Washington revised its opinion of him. Secretary of State John Foster Dulles canceled orders to shift support away from him; Diem was now America's leader for South Vietnam.

Diem immediately reaped benefits from his new stature. The United States gave South Vietnam money to pay all its government and military expenses as well as enough to cover the south's trade deficit. The army was the most expensive: Diem spent eight dollars of every ten dollars of American aid on the police and the military.

The United States was concerned that the south would be attacked by North Vietnam. Earlier, in September 1954, Secretary of State Dulles had negotiated an entirely new security pact with Great Britain, France, Australia, New Zealand, Thailand, and Pakistan known as the Southeast Asia Treaty Organization, or SEATO, whose members were pledged to protect Saigon from foreign aggression.

But at this stage Diem was troubled by opponents in the south more than by the threat of an invasion from the north. In 1955 he launched an expensive "Anti-Communist

Denunciation Campaign" aimed at eliminating those who opposed his regime. He passed laws allowing him to imprison anyone he considered a threat to his government or to the security of the nation. Often the people arrested were tortured, and many were killed. Records from that period show that most of the people accused of favoring communism were Vietnamese who had fought against French colonialism and were not happy with Diem's undemocratic rule. Violence led to more violence, and a campaign of terror spread throughout the south, lasting through 1959.

In October 1955 Emperor Bao Dai, living comfortably in exile in Paris, issued a statement condemning Diem's "police methods and personal dictatorship [which] must be brought to an end. . . . I can no longer continue to lend my name and my authority to a man who will drag [Vietnam] into ruin."

Diem's response was swift. He promoted himself to chief of state, then held elections at the end of the year to approve his action and a new constitution. He won 98 percent of the vote by rigging the elections. Neither Bao Dai's name nor his authority was necessary for Diem. He had altered the constitution to make the emperor irrelevant.

A Deadline Passes

Diem's approach to the nationwide elections mandated by the Geneva Accords was entirely different. In late 1955 a U.S. intelligence estimate concluded that "Diem will almost certainly not agree to hold national elections for the unification of Vietnam by July 1956 [the Geneva deadline]. . . . Diem will probably seek to bind the U.S. more specifically to the defense of Vietnam." Other documents show that the United States thought the best idea was to "postpone" elections. Diem, however, wanted to cancel them. He said the government of South Vietnam did not sign the accords and therefore was not bound by them.

Diem was opposed to the elections because he was convinced he would lose. He would not be able to cheat in national balloting supervised by an international organization, as he had in the recent southern election. He and most other Vietnamese were convinced that Ho Chi Minh and the Viet Minh would be the overwhelming victors. From his palatial residence in Saigon, Diem ignored pleas from the communists in the north to agree to the elections and implement the accords.

Stymied by Diem, the Hanoi government petitioned the commission set up by the Geneva Accords to enforce the holding of elections in North and South Vietnam. The two chairmen of the commission were from the governments of Great Britain and the Soviet Union; they agreed that the accords required the two Vietnamese governments to meet and prepare for "free, nationwide elections in Vietnam under the supervision of an International Commission with a view to the reestablishment of the national unity of Vietnam."

But the July 1956 deadline came, and nothing happened.

In Saigon Diem convened a new National Assembly, which approved his new constitution. Confident once the election deadline had passed, Diem ordered the arrest of more South Vietnamese who opposed his rule. By the end of 1956, some 20,000 people were in camps for political prisoners in the south.

For the time being Diem's strategy worked. The communists in the north were unable to do anything about Diem's refusal to hold elections. The United States allowed Diem to avoid the elections, and the Soviet Union, North Vietnam's chief ally, tried to avoid confrontation with the United States by suggesting that both Vietnams be admitted to the United Nations, in effect giving their approval to a divided country.

Ho Chi Minh and his government felt betrayed on all sides. They lost faith in the Geneva Accords and from that moment on became cynical about the power of international law. But the communists did not contemplate an immediate military attack on the south to bring about unification by force. They felt they were too weak to go up against Diem because he was so well armed by the Americans. At the same time they believed Diem was so unpopular that he could be undermined through political agitation. The northern communists secretly sent their followers in the south a new plan called "The Path of Revolution in the South." The southerners were told to be patient and follow "the peaceful line." They were not to fight against Diem's police or the military but to have faith in the "people's will for peace."

In the north the communists, realizing that the division of the country was not temporary, started to establish their rule over the countryside and to build up their army in preparation for war to unify the country. Now the communist ideology, which had worked so well in organizing the war to overthrow French colonialism and assert Vietnamese independence, proved disastrous when applied to the north's economic structure.

Much of the north had been ruined by the war against the French, which had barely affected the south. Moreover, some noncommunist North Vietnamese who had fled after the signing of the Geneva Accords had deliberately destroyed factories, hospitals, and other important facilities to make sure that the north was severely crippled. Finally, the division of the country had robbed the north of the food it needed from the south, especially rice.

Ho Chi Minh used communist ideology to try to solve these economic problems, especially how to grow rice in the north. In 1956 he began a program of land reform. With unthinking rigidity, the North Vietnamese followed communist doctrine requiring that they "eliminate" wealthy landowners and distribute land to the peasants, even though there were very few rich landlords in the north. The Vietnamese communists killed thousands of would-be farmers accused of being landowners and peasants accused of working for the French.

A few months later Ho Chi Minh publicly admitted that his reform plan had spawned terror, and he apologized, ordering that the reform system be modified. But the communist system was put in place. There were no basic democratic rights. Only communist literature and communist views were allowed. Only one political party, the communist, was allowed. At the time, the brutality of communism was camouflaged. In the north there was an overall notion of equality; everyone seemed to share the same hardships. The monolithic communist party system did create a shared sense of mission and the organization needed for the next phase of fighting. Moreover, the Vietnamese had never known democracy. The hope was that with peace all these rules and restrictions would be relaxed.

In the south Diem was in a good position to create the

"showpiece of democracy" the Americans wanted as a contrast to the communist rule in the north. From 1956 until the end of President Eisenhower's term in office in 1960, the United States gave South Vietnam more than a billion dollars in economic and military aid. But Diem's government was anything but a democracy: there was little individual freedom, the people did not participate directly in the government, and the peasants received none of the promised aid or reforms. The historian Frances FitzGerald wrote, "As the Diem regime grew older, the administration began to take on more and more of the properties of a sponge. Money, plans, and programs poured into it and nothing came out the other end."

Diem was building a personal kingdom, not a democracy. South Vietnamese officers were trained at considerable expense in the United States, but if Diem considered them disloyal they never served where they might threaten him. The United States also gave Diem's government money for programs to alleviate poverty. However, Diem's major "reform" was to dissolve the elected village councils and appoint his own friends as leaders of the villages, where they were often strangers. Diem's police prevented the people from protesting against this charade of reform and democracy by imprisoning or murdering opponents, including communists.

Finally a group of Saigon intellectuals publicly asked Diem to change his ways before it was too late. In the "Manifesto of the Eighteen" they began by reminding Diem of the early hopes for his regime: "The people hoped no longer to be compelled to pay homage to one regime in the morning and to another at night, not to be prey to the cruelties and oppression of one faction; no longer to be treated as coolies; no longer to be at the mercy of the monopolies; no longer to have to endure the depredations of corrupt and despotic civil servants. In one word, the people hoped to live in security at last, under a regime which would give them a little bit of justice and liberty."

After this eloquent recital of old hopes, the writers described what Diem had accomplished instead: "Continuous arrests fill the jails and prisons to the rafters. . . . Public opinion and the press are reduced to silence. . . . Political parties and religious sects have been eliminated. . . . New oppressions [have been inflicted on] the population without protecting it [from communism]."

Eisenhower's America

Diem's betrayal of democracy meant little in the United States, where Vietnam was not yet seen as a burning issue, even though South Vietnam received the fifth largest amount of American foreign aid.

In the late 1950s, while the rest of the world was either recovering from the Second World War or trying to industrialize, America was building new suburbs with split-level houses, new schools, ribbons of freeways, and the first shopping malls. This was an era of supreme American confidence, an era that celebrated the new, young lifestyle of Elvis Presley and rock and roll, blue jeans and leather jackets, innocence and wide-open spaces. America was at the peak of its world power. Its only rival was the Soviet Union, whose bleak communist doctrine paled alongside America's open energy.

Glossy American magazines portrayed Diem as part of the American dream, the man who had wrought "miracles" in South Vietnam. Diem was fighting communism, still a single, unified threat in the American mind. Communist Russia and its eastern European satellites, along with China, North Korea, and North Vietnam, were portrayed as a solitary bloc of poor but clever nations threatening the free world. Diem was "our man" in South Vietnam, fighting for that free world. And American politicians instinctively accepted this simple ideology. To them Vietnam was one of those nations — like Germany and Korea — tragically divided by the Cold War into communist and noncommunist halves. America's responsibility was to defend the noncommunist halves from their communist rivals.

America's anticommunism grew out of bounds in the 1950s, but it was solidly based on the frightening turn of events in eastern Europe. The Soviet Union imposed a brutal dictatorship over all the countries it occupied following World War II, dividing the European continent in half. Refugees fleeing from Poland, Czechoslovakia, Hungary, and eastern Germany told stories of the Stalinist terror, including show trials, secret police, and a complete loss of freedom and dignity. The Iron Curtain dividing western and eastern Europe motivated American reaction in Vietnam, for better and for worse. The United States had become the policeman.

3

TAKING OVER FROM
THE FRENCH

It all depends on Diem's effectiveness. . . .
The 30 percent chance is that we would wind up
like the French in 1954; white men can't
win this kind of fight.
— *William P. Bundy,*
acting assistant secretary of defense, 1961

Kennedy and Diem

THE DECADE OF THE 1960s began full of high expectations
in the United States and troubled premonitions in Vietnam.

The North Vietnamese communists believed there
could be no turning back from a military confrontation with
Diem. In 1959 Ho Chi Minh decided that his hopes for a
political end to the conflict through the Geneva Accords
were unrealistic. He gave permission to the southern communists to fight back against Diem's police. For the Vietnamese communists this marked a new stage in their long
resistance and revolution.

The United States in 1960 elected a young president
who spoke of new American challenges and a promising

future. The charismatic John F. Kennedy, Diem's old friend, won the election by a slim margin but immediately charmed the American public. When Kennedy replaced the wise, deliberate, balding Eisenhower, his tousled hair came to symbolize the new image he hoped his country would project. He appealed to the idealism of the country, most notably with his creation of the Peace Corps, volunteers sent out by the government to teach skills to developing countries around the world, like secular missionaries.

More than anything else, Kennedy wanted to offer young Americans a new beginning. With his handsome wife, Jacqueline, and his brilliant advisers, he exuded an easy confidence. No problem seemed too great for the Kennedy administration, which had pledged to conquer the New Frontier.

These fresh beginnings were embarked upon with little reflection; Vietnam became the most costly example of Kennedy's refusal to study problems in depth and look for the best solution regardless of past assumptions. Kennedy's advisers accepted the Eisenhower administration's judgment that Vietnam was on the cutting edge of the free world's fight against communism. They rejected the interpretation that the Vietnamese were continuing their fight against French colonialism, now transmuted into a civil war between communists and vaguely defined noncommunists.

Vietnam was not Kennedy's first crisis. The invasion of the Bay of Pigs in Fidel Castro's communist Cuba seized the president's attention at the beginning of his term. The CIA had led Kennedy into that illegal adventure, in which Cuban exiles were sent to attack the island and suffered a humiliating public defeat. Thereafter Kennedy was wary of the CIA and the leaders of the armed forces, the Joint Chiefs of Staff, whom he also blamed for the fiasco. At this early stage Kennedy lost confidence in his military leaders and began accepting political judgments over military. This proved to have profound repercussions for his Vietnam policy.

In June 1961, a few months after the Bay of Pigs invasion, President Kennedy met Soviet leader Nikita Khrushchev in Vienna, Austria. Khrushchev taunted the young American leader and told him directly that the Soviet Union supported "wars of national liberation." In other words, the Soviet Union would encourage revolutionary wars against foreign powers. The Vietnamese communists believed they were fighting such a war against American imperialism. Kennedy understood Khrushchev's message and took it as a challenge.

That fall the southern communists' war of national liberation in Vietnam broke out on a new scale. Earlier the communists had concentrated on convincing peasants and farmers in the south to support them by emphasizing Diem's corruption and demonstrating how his reforms had actually harmed them rather than bringing them any benefits. Diem's undercover police were tracking down the communists and routinely capturing and killing them, so in 1959 the party leaders in the north gave the southern communists permission to go after Diem's police. In 1959 they killed 1,200 officials of Diem's regime, and in 1961 another 4,000. The North began sending aid and troops to the southern communists: a guerrilla insurgency was under way.

President Kennedy turned his attention to what seemed to be a new stage in the war for Vietnam. Earlier he had resisted advice to beef up America's military presence of 685 advisers in the south, but now he sent 400 Special Forces troops, known as the Green Berets, to train the South Vietnamese soldiers in "counterinsurgency" warfare.

In the fall of 1961, when the communists captured a provincial capital in the south, several of Kennedy's advisers urged him to further increase American involvement in the Vietnamese conflict. General Maxwell D. Taylor, Kennedy's military adviser, went to South Vietnam and reported back to the president, "[I am] recommending the introduction of a U.S. military force into South Vietnam. I have reached the conclusion that this is an essential action if we are to reverse the present downward trend of events."

Taylor stressed the positive, saying that introducing troops would "provide a U.S. military presence capable of raising national morale and of showing to Southeast Asia the seriousness of the U.S. intent to resist a communist takeover."

But he did not hide the problems that could result from sending American troops into combat in Vietnam. "If the first contingent is not enough to accomplish the necessary results, it will be difficult to resist the pressure to reinforce. If the ultimate result sought is the closing of the frontiers and the cleanup of the insurgents within South Vietnam, there is no limit to our possible commitment (unless we attack the source in Hanoi)." Taylor underlined the risk: "The introduction of U.S. forces may increase tensions and risk escalation into a major war in Asia."

In effect, Taylor was outlining the two faces of what became the Vietnam War. The first, the idea that soldiers and bullets could act as symbols of America's unstinting support for the south, was a dream. The second, the fear of an escalation into a major war, proved to be realistic. Soldiers could not be sent into a war and told to act as symbols or morale boosters. They had to be sent as soldiers fighting to win. And sending a superpower's army across the world to Vietnam ensured that the conflict would escalate.

Taylor's recommendation to send American troops was buttressed by a separate memorandum from Kennedy's secretary of defense, Robert S. McNamara. He provided the strategic rationale for this escalation, the domino theory. If American troops were sent into South Vietnam, the country could be protected from communism, he wrote; if not, "the rest of mainland Southeast Asia and Indonesia [would fall to communism]. . . . The chances are against, probably sharply against, preventing that fall by any measures short of the introduction of U.S. troops on a substantial scale." McNamara tried to push Kennedy "to commit the U.S. to the clear objective of preventing the fall of South Vietnam to Communism and [demonstrate] that we support this commitment by the necessary military actions."

Kennedy thought Taylor's and McNamara's recommendations were premature. He accepted Taylor's argument that the United States had to stand up to communist aggression in South Vietnam, but he said no to sending combat troops.

Instead the president embraced the concept of counterinsurgency to fight the communist guerrillas in the south. The southern communists, with help from the North Vietnamese, were fighting the Diem regime with sabotage, infiltration, and assassinations, while trying to win over the population with political education and mass propaganda, making the war as much a political rivalry as a military confrontation.

Kennedy's approach was to send the Green Berets to train the South Vietnamese soldiers to search out the communist insurgents and kill them; at the same time he tried to match the communists' political appeal by funding generous aid projects and establishing political education programs that demonstrated the evils of communism. American advisers were sent to instruct Diem on how to transform his corrupt regime into one that benefited the common people. But very few of the Green Berets or the advisers knew Vietnam's language or history or the issues facing the country. The Americans and their South Vietnamese partners literally could not understand each other from the beginning, and the best of intentions could not surmount this basic inability to communicate or to agree on what was best for Vietnam.

The president agreed to Taylor's other recommendations to dramatically increase American aid and to raise the number of American military advisers in Vietnam to 12,000. In Kennedy's view this was part of the counterinsurgency program.

This was not an innocent compromise. By raising the number of military advisers to 12,000, Kennedy knowingly violated the Geneva Accords' armistice provisions, a step the Eisenhower administration had refused to take. American law has never accepted the idea that just because an enemy breaks a law the United States can do the same. Now Kennedy had discarded the one international agreement that limited American involvement in Vietnam. In speaking to a friend Kennedy admitted this, saying, "The trouble is, we are violating the Geneva agreement. Not as much as the North Vietnamese are, but we're violating it."

The president gave a different explanation to the American public. The State Department released a government policy statement, known as a "white paper," entitled "A Threat to the Peace: North Viet Nam's Effort to Conquer South Viet Nam." The paper's argument rested on the deceptive premise that North Vietnam was a foreign country invading the sovereign nation of South Vietnam, a concept the international community did not accept. In fact, North and South Vietnam were two halves of a single country fighting a civil war.

In December 1960 the communists created the National Liberation Front, or NLF, in the south to present as broad an appeal as possible against the regime in Saigon and to counter the claims of Diem and the Americans that the southern communists were puppets of the north. The NLF, which was known as the Viet Cong, was made up of South Vietnamese of many political persuasions, occupations, and backgrounds who said that they were independent of the north but in agreement with it on most issues. This was a complicated subterfuge, largely because the northern communists did control those in the south in most important ways. However, the northerners did accommodate their ideas to views held by the southerners. Indeed, it was the southerners who convinced the north that it was time to do battle with the Diem regime rather than allow Diem's police to hunt down and murder more southern communists.

The NLF's first published manifesto opened with a citation from the 1954 Geneva Accords recognizing "the sovereignty, independence, unity and territorial integrity of Vietnam." By this the NLF meant one country made up of all the factions opposed to the Saigon regime but controlled by a single communist party headquartered in the north. The manifesto also singled out the United States as the chief enemy. "The American imperialists, who had in the past helped the French colonialists to massacre our people, have now replaced the French in enslaving the southern part of our country through a disguised colonial regime."

One of Kennedy's most trusted and astute advisers came to a similar conclusion, in far less belligerent prose, at roughly the same time. The president had asked John Kenneth Galbraith, a renowned economist, to travel through South Vietnam on his way to New Delhi, where he would serve as the U.S. ambassador to India. Galbraith's assessment of Diem, his army, and the government was that they were "a can of snakes." And he predicted that "we shall replace the French as the colonial force in the area and bleed as the French did." This was another warning ignored, one that echoed sadly through American history.

Indeed, in 1960 Diem had to thwart a revolt by some military officers who wanted to overthrow him. A U.S. State Department intelligence report had predicted this revolt and warned that Diem's army officers were upset by "the worsening of the internal security, the promotion of incompetent officers . . . and [Diem's] political favoritism." Specifically, the report said the officer corps deeply resented Diem's brother, Ngo Dinh Nhu, for his powerful and corrupting control over the government. The attempted revolt failed within forty-eight hours and left hundreds dead. Diem reacted by shutting himself up in the presidential palace, trusting fewer and fewer people and relying more heavily on his brother and other family members. The Diem family government was looking very much like the old imperial court.

First Steps

In 1962 the United States joined eleven countries in signing accords to make Laos a neutral nation in increasingly troubled Indochina. Kennedy knew that the communists in neighboring North Vietnam were using mountain trails in Laos to send supplies and men to their comrades in the south. The maze of trails that snaked through Laos, Vietnam, and, later, Cambodia became known as the Ho Chi Minh Trail. It was the spine of the communists' war effort, their supply and communication link. Still, Kennedy decided that the small nation of Laos was not vital to American national security. In the American president's eyes, that distinction belonged to Vietnam. The United States continued to send military men, money, machines, and supplies to South Vietnam.

As the U.S. involvement increased, the American public began wondering what Kennedy had in mind in Vietnam. How could American troops be acting only as advisers when thousands were being sent to a country fighting an all-out guerrilla war? At a 1962 press conference Kennedy answered that question by saying that American soldiers were told to fire back only in self-defense. Other officials acknowledged that the advisers often trained the South Vietnamese "under combat conditions."

The casualty figure that year showed how routinely Americans were caught in combat. In 1961 only 14 American soldiers were killed or wounded; in 1962 the figure was 109.

Kennedy and his advisers emphasized that assistance for South Vietnam's military was only part of their counterinsurgency program. They knew that Diem had to defeat the communists with a wise political program as well as with military might, and they believed Diem would allow them to turn South Vietnam into that illusory showpiece of democracy and the free market. To that end the president approved the following recommendations in 1962:

> Undertake economic programs having both a short-term immediate impact as well as ones which contribute to the longer-range economic viability of the country.
>
> Assist [South Vietnam] to accelerate its public information program to help develop a broad public understanding of the actions required to combat the communist insurgents and to build public confidence.

The centerpiece of these new programs was the Strategic Hamlet Program. This was an ambitious idea to reorganize village life so that the South Vietnamese would not join, aid, or be coerced by the NLF, known generally as the Viet Cong. Under this program, the people of several small villages would be brought together in one large hamlet. A moat would be dug all around the new hamlet, and bamboo spears would be stuck in the moat to frighten away would-be assailants. Armed guards were posted at the gates. The idea was a twentieth-century adaptation of medieval fortification. In return for moving their homes and villages, the farmers were to be rewarded with generous American aid.

This severe program of forcing families to give up their

homes for the uncertain safety of a strategic hamlet was a response to specific tactics of the Viet Cong. Throughout the south the Viet Cong were moving swiftly, secretly from village to village. Often they were able to convince the villagers to support them against Diem and to give them food and shelter as well as information and protection from the police.

The Viet Cong compared this practice of infiltrating local villages and staying on the move to the movement of fish swimming through water. Ho Chi Minh reminded his soldiers that the only way they could be camouflaged in the villages was if "the army and the people are like fish and water. . . . The soldiers must not steal even a needle or a bit of thread belonging to the people." Generally the Viet Cong followed Ho Chi Minh's advice and treated the villagers fairly, especially when compared to the Diem officials.

But the villagers understood they could not be neutral in the conflict between the Viet Cong and the Saigon regime. Although the Viet Cong may have been less brutal and insensitive than Diem's solders and officials, they *were* armed soldiers. Villagers understood they had to give token cooperation to the Viet Cong or the government to avoid reprisals.

Sir Robert Thompson, an Englishman, had invented the Strategic Hamlet Program as a way of closing off villages to outsiders, thus separating the guerrillas from the people. But Thompson's idea was based on his experience in Malaysia, where the Chinese guerrillas were of a different race from the Malay villagers. In Vietnam, not only were the insurgents of the same race, they were often from the same neighborhood and the same class. If Viet Cong soldiers slipped into a strategic hamlet, they would look and act like the other villagers and go undetected. They could attack their targets — Diem's police, soldiers, and spies — and sneak out again.

Diem's brother and chief counselor, Ngo Dinh Nhu, was enthusiastic about the program because he believed it offered the possibility of finally cornering the Viet Cong. As Nhu explained, "Since we did not know where the enemy was, ten times we launched a military operation, nine times we missed the Viet Cong, and the tenth time we struck right on the head of the [civilian] population." According to Nhu's logic, anyone caught outside a strategic hamlet would be considered a communist. The Americans saw the program as a way of reforming the countryside, of offering villagers a safe area where they could be convinced that democracy was a better alternative to communism. But the American idea was deformed in practice, and South Vietnamese officials made even more arbitrary arrests of villagers suspected of being communists because they were not in the new hamlets.

The peasants' lives grew worse. After moving into a strategic hamlet, one villager recalled, "I had two hectares of rice in the old village. Now it is ripe and the grain falls into the paddy mud. I cannot harvest it. There are men here with guns who tell me that we must dig a ditch. . . . In the bottom of that ditch there must be a fence of barbed wire. When it is finished I can return to harvest my rice. But my rice will be gone. Who will feed my family?"

The Strategic Hamlet Program backfired. One South Vietnamese official said, "Asking the villagers to dig a hole around their village in the hot sun while their rice became overripe and fell to the ground was perfect propaganda for the Viet Cong. Instead of separating the population from the Viet Cong, we were making Viet Cong."

That observation was repeated in an end-of-the-year report by the U.S. State Department. "The Viet Cong has expanded the size and enhanced the capability and organization of its guerrilla force," the report said, even though the South Vietnamese government had "paid more attention to political, economic and social counterinsurgency measures."

By the end of 1962 the communists controlled or influenced nearly half the villages in the south, the Americans discovered. Worse, the communists were making inroads in the cities, which had been thought of as Diem's strongholds. The American report continued: "Viet Cong influence has almost certainly improved in urban areas not only through subversion and terrorism but also because of its propaganda appeal to the increasingly frustrated non-communist and anti-Diem element."

These findings raised basic questions for the United States. If half the villages of the south were sympathetic to the communists, and if communists were winning over the sophisticated residents of Saigon, Hue, and Da Nang, what was the rationale for the American buildup? But the State Department report did not pose that question. Instead it discussed the prospect of a successful coup d'état against the Diem regime: "There are also reports that important military and civilian officials continue to participate in coup plots. . . . A coup could occur at any time, but would be more likely if the fight against the communists goes badly." Thus the assessment ended, after persuasively demonstrating that the fight had already gone badly.

This was the year that the United States introduced the helicopter into the war in Vietnam.

Assassinations

On May 5, 1963, the South Vietnamese government sponsored a huge celebration to mark the twenty-fifth anniversary of the ordination of Diem's oldest brother as a Roman Catholic bishop. The festivities were held in the old capital of Hue, and all over the city the official Roman Catholic flag of the Vatican flew from poles in public and private quarters.

Two days later the Buddhists of Hue began preparations to celebrate the birthday of Lord Buddha on May 8. They decorated the city as the Catholics had, flying their own Buddhist flags. But Diem's police immediately stepped in and reminded the Buddhists of a law forbidding the display of religious flags in public places. The Buddhists were ordered to remove all their flags from public places and to fly them only from pagodas and religious buildings. When the Buddhists refused, citing the Catholics' display just two days earlier, the police took down several of the flags and told the Buddhists to finish the job. The police said they were acting at the strong urging of the archbishop, Diem's brother.

Buddha's birthday became a day of peaceful protest. Twenty thousand Buddhists gathered to demonstrate against the government for continually favoring the minority Catholics over the Buddhists. The head monk delivered scathing attacks against the government's open hypocrisy. One glance around the city, with its imperial tombs and gates and its pagodas crowned with Oriental roofs curving up toward heaven, was proof that the city's Buddhist tradition was old and strong, stronger than the whim of a Catholic archbishop, even if he was the president's brother.

Toward evening a crowd gathered outside the city's small radio station to demand that the manager broadcast the head monk's speech. Afraid to make such a decision on his own, the manager called in the army. Shortly after the soldiers arrived, two explosions shattered the darkness. In response, the soldiers threw hand grenades. Seven people were killed, their bodies torn apart by the grenades, and one child was near death.

The Buddhist Crisis had begun.

Diem was ill prepared for the crisis. He had shut himself off from all but a few family members and friends, whose presence in the closed government circle was a big part of the problem. As he faced this challenge from the Buddhists, he had no friends who dared to tell him what trouble his government faced, and he had too many enemies who spoke of him and his family with bitterness.

The Buddhist Crisis began with Diem's family. Under the influence of his brother, the archbishop, Diem had formally dedicated South Vietnam to the Virgin Mary in 1959, even though fewer than 10 percent of the people were Catholics. The archbishop's repeated demands that the president favor the Catholic minority had culminated in the flag incident at Hue.

Diem's sister-in-law, Madame Ngo Dinh Nhu, added to the political crisis. Beautiful, outspoken, and mean-spirited, Madame Nhu had become South Vietnam's unofficial First Lady. Diem, a bachelor, had invited his brother and wife to move into the presidential palace when he came into power, and Madame Nhu used her position to promote a bizarre collection of government policies, supposedly for the good of Vietnamese womanhood. Under her influence, divorce, abortion, contraception, and nightclub dancing were outlawed. She flaunted her own femininity by wearing extremely tight clothes, painting her nails bright red, and carrying a pistol to encourage women to defend themselves. She was also amassing a small fortune by demanding bribes and shares in corrupt trade. Shrewdly, she sent her money overseas.

During the 1963 Buddhist Crisis, Madame Nhu came into her own. After the deaths outside the Hue radio station, the Buddhists published a list of demands, for equal legal status with the Catholics, full freedom of worship, and compensation for the families of the victims killed on May 8. The government was near a compromise when Madame Nhu spoiled the negotiations by declaring that she believed the Buddhists had been infiltrated by communists.

On June 7 she issued a statement in the name of her Women's Solidarity League implying that the Buddhist protests were controlled by the communists. Four days later a seventy-three-year-old Buddhist monk sat down at a busy Saigon intersection, calmly poured gasoline over himself, lit a match, and set his body aflame, all the while chanting prayers. In five minutes he was dead. The monk used one of the few forms of violent protest sanctioned by his religion, committing suicide by fire, to protest Diem's treatment of the Buddhists.

An American reporter's photograph of the scene, published in newspapers all over the world, shows flames breaking like ocean waves over the monk's shaven head and thin body. The world was horrified. What conditions could be so awful that a man would burn himself to death to protest against his government?

Madame Nhu turned the tragedy into a grievous insult by describing the monk's death as a "barbecue." The Buddhist Crisis ballooned into a challenge to Diem's rule. For the rest of the summer he tried to find a compromise with the Buddhists, as the Americans had practically ordered him to do. But the Buddhist demands grew and became nonnegotiable. The police jailed Buddhist protesters in Saigon, Da Lat, Hue, and Nha Trang. A second monk burned himself to death, then a third. Finally, a nun set herself aflame.

In Rome the pope appealed to Diem's government to be tolerant and to end this confrontation. The pope's representative in Saigon asked for kindness between the people of different religions. Diem ignored the pope's advice and listened to his brother instead, who counseled confrontation. On August 21 Diem's combat police and troops from a special force stormed Buddhist pagodas in a series of audacious midnight raids. Like Christian churches, the pagodas were considered safe from attack. But that summer the pagodas had been turned into headquarters of revolt where Buddhists plotted protests and antigovernment actions.

Diem's police arrested hundreds of Buddhists in the raids. The Americans were furious; he was supposed to be fighting communist guerrillas, not Buddhist pacifists.

Several of Diem's officers considered making another attempt at a coup. A South Vietnamese general secretly informed a CIA agent of a plot by several officers and asked how the United States would react. The agent turned to his superiors in Washington for an answer, and the American government took the first step toward approving plans to overthrow Diem.

How did the United States reach this decision? Who promoted the coup? Who warned against it? The answers are in the secret messages between Saigon and Washington, which have now become public. The cable traffic was between the U.S. Embassy in Saigon, the White House, and the State Department; between the military advisory group in South Vietnam and the Joint Chiefs of Staff at the Pentagon; and between the CIA liaison in Saigon and CIA headquarters in a suburb of Washington.

In this crucial period in autumn 1963, President Kennedy acted on the prejudices against the Joint Chiefs of Staff that he had built up because of the Bay of Pigs disaster. He and his closest advisers repeatedly accepted the judgments of the newly arrived ambassador to South Vietnam, Henry Cabot Lodge, over those of General Paul D. Harkins, the head of the military assistance command in Saigon.

Lodge had been Richard M. Nixon's vice presidential running mate in the 1960 election, which Kennedy had won. Earlier Kennedy had defeated Lodge in an election for senator from Massachusetts. Yet when Kennedy, a Democrat, appointed Lodge, a Republican, as ambassador to Saigon, it was considered a smart move to ensure Republican support for Kennedy's Vietnam policy.

Lodge had arrived in Saigon with no commitments to Diem or to America's policy of building democratic institutions in South Vietnam. General Harkins and other Americans who knew something about the state of affairs in the south cautioned Lodge that the generals plotting the coup were even weaker than Diem. Lodge did not agree.

One of the first messages regarding the proposed coup was from the CIA in Washington, instructing its Saigon agent to tell the plotters that "if Nhus [the president's brother and Madame Nhu] do not go and if the Buddhist situation is not redressed as indicated, we would find it impossible to continue military and economic support. It is hoped bloodshed can be avoided or reduced to absolute minimum." The American response, then, was to encourage the general to go ahead with the coup. This commitment marked America's full entry into the war.

Three days later Ambassador Lodge cabled Washington: "We are launched on a course from which there is no respectable turning back: the overthrow of the Diem government. . . . The chance of bringing off a Generals' coup depends on them to some extent; but it depends at least as much on us."

That same day Washington answered Lodge's cable in brisk bureaucratic language: "The [United States] will support a coup which has good chance of succeeding but plans no direct involvement of U.S. armed forces."

Without saying so directly, the U.S. government had become an active partner in an illegal coup against Diem. Lodge preferred to view the coup as the best way to "reform" the government. He cabled back to Washington: "The best chance [of reform] is by the generals taking over the government lock, stock and barrel."

The generals, however, hesitated and did not attempt to go ahead with their coup in August. When that news reached Washington, officials gathered to reconsider their position. At a top-secret meeting everyone agreed that the Diem regime was corrupt and ineffective, and one official argued that because of this the United States should get out of Vietnam instead of plunging in deeper by supporting a coup. According to the notes from that meeting the official said, "If we undertake to live with this repressive regime, with its bayonets at every street corner and its transparent negotiations with puppet bonzes [monks], we are going to be thrown out of the country in six months. . . . At this juncture it would be better for us to make the decision to get out honorably." The others at the meeting strongly disagreed.

President Kennedy was worried. He sent his secretary of defense and the chairman of the Joint Chiefs of Staff on a study mission to Vietnam, asking them to clarify the situation. They reported back: "There is no solid evidence of the possibility of a successful coup, although assassination of Diem or Nhu is always a possibility." They recommended that the United States take "no initiative . . . to encourage actively a change in government. Our policy should be to seek urgently to identify and build contacts with an alternative leadership if and when it appears."

Did that mean the United States should resume talking to generals who were plotting another coup? Did "building contacts" mean telling the generals that the United States wanted to be kept abreast of coup plans? Three days after that report was filed, several South Vietnamese generals again spoke to the CIA agent in Saigon. Ambassador Lodge cabled Washington, "The Generals were aware the situation is deteriorating rapidly and that action to change the Government must be taken or the war will be lost to the Viet Cong because the Government no longer has the support of the people." Lodge reported that the coup plotters said they "need American assurances that the U.S. will not, repeat not, attempt to thwart this plan."

Kennedy, trying to convince himself that the United States was not an active participant in the plot, cabled back: "We repeat that this effort is not repeat not to be aimed at active promotion of coup but only at surveillance and readiness."

The president may have believed that the United States

was not involved in the coup, but simply by knowing about it and not warning Diem, who was an ally and a legitimate head of government, the United States was an accomplice in the coup. Because of its control over the south's economy and the military aid it sent, the United States had become the major power in the south.

Lodge reassured Kennedy that the American role was hidden. On October 25, 1963, he cabled Washington: "I believe that our involvement to date through [the CIA agent] is still within the realm of plausible denial. [I will] disavow [the agent] at any time it may serve the national interest." Lodge warned that the coup was imminent: "The best evidence available to the Embassy, which I grant you is not as complete as we would like it, is that General Don and the other generals involved with him are seriously attempting to effect a change in the government."

Soon afterward General Harkins, the head of the military assistance group in Saigon, cabled his boss, General Taylor of the Joint Chiefs of Staff, to protest Lodge's enthusiasm for the coup. Diem's government should be reformed, he wrote, not overthrown. Harkins pleaded that the United States should respect the laws forbidding active participation in the overthrow of a foreign government, which Lodge seemed to be ignoring, and pointed out that the plotting generals had not shown the "strength of character of Diem." He said, "There are no Generals qualified to take over in my opinion. I am not a Diem man per se. I certainly see the faults in his character. I am here to back 14 million [South Vietnamese] people in their fight against communism and it just happens that Diem is their leader at this time. Most of the Generals I have talked to agree they can go along with Diem, all say it's the Nhu family they are opposed to."

Harkins had known the South Vietnamese generals for nearly two years; Lodge had been in the country for only two months. Realizing this, the administration wavered. Washington sent a confusing cable to Lodge asking if he might be able to stop the coup. It read: "Believe our attitude to coup group can still have decisive effect on its decisions. We believe that what we say to coup group can produce delay of coup and that betrayal of coup plans to Diem is not repeat not our only way of stopping coup."

Lodge answered, "Do not think we have the power to delay or discourage coup." His cable concluded, "General Harkins has read this and does not concur." But at this point Harkins's disapproval did not matter; the coup was only hours away.

On November 1, 1963, the South Vietnamese generals staged their coup, and the American CIA agent was in the midst of the action. When Diem refused to give in to their demands, the generals surrounded the presidential palace. Diem then telephoned Lodge and asked, "What is the attitude of the United States?"

Lodge said, "I do not feel well enough informed to be able to tell you. I have heard the shooting, but am not acquainted with all the facts."

Diem, knowing Lodge was lying, implored, "You must have some general ideas."

Lodge, who wanted nothing more than to see the coup succeed, made a feeble offer: "If I can do anything for your physical safety, please call me."

With this, Diem knew that his rule was over. He and his brother Nhu escaped through a secret passage and fled to Cholon, the city's Chinatown, where they hid in a Catholic church. The following day they turned themselves in to the military authorities in return for safe passage out of the country; however, inside the armored personnel carrier that was supposed to take them to safety, they were murdered at point blank range. Madame Nhu escaped harm because she was out of the country.

Hours later, when President Kennedy was told that Diem and his brother had died during the coup, he turned ashen. Diem's assassination brought home the enormity of the president's actions. The United States had encouraged and supported the coup and was implicated in that crime. It was also committed to the coup's plotters, who had killed Diem after promising him freedom in exile.

Until this time American policy toward Vietnam could have been misinterpreted as well-meaning if wrong. But after the assassination of Diem, a corner had been turned.

Three weeks later President John F. Kennedy was assassinated on the streets of Dallas, Texas.

4

CROSSING THE LINE

Aᶠᵗᵉʳ ᵗʰᵉ ᵐⁱˡⁱᵗᵃʳʸ ᵒᶠᶠⁱᶜᵉʳˢ overthrew and murdered Ngo Dinh Diem, they set up a ruling junta for South Vietnam and relaxed many of the severe restrictions Diem had imposed. In Saigon and much of the countryside the people celebrated, creating a false spring of hope amid the growing fears of a larger war.

Madame Nhu's ban on singing was lifted, and the South Vietnamese could again hear the melancholy, sentimental songs they adored. They could dance and meet their friends with far less fear of being arrested as "troublemakers." Hundreds of adults and students who had been detained without trial were released. On returning home, some told stories of being interrogated all night, of solitary confinement in cramped cells, and of physical beatings. Doing away with Madame Nhu's absurd prohibitions and releasing people from confinement was the junta's easiest success. Far more difficult would be fighting the war and ruling the country.

The twelve officers who ran South Vietnam under the name of the Military Revolutionary Council, led by Duong Van Minh, or Big Minh, were inexperienced as political leaders. They disagreed among themselves on how to lead the country. Quickly the sense of hope was overtaken by a wave of chaos.

The junta, wanting to end the squabbling among the South Vietnamese, invited the disaffected religious groups, from Buddhists to Cao Daists, to take part in the new regime instead of fighting it. In an effort to make the farmers and peasants feel a part of the society, they officially ended the despised Strategic Hamlet Program.

Junta leaders even wanted to ask the noncommunist members of the Viet Cong to leave that group and become part of their society. With half of South Vietnam effectively under the control of the Viet Cong, the junta leaders searched for practical ways to reassert Saigon's authority. They felt they could divide and conquer their rivals through the close ties they had maintained to the noncommunist members of the Viet Cong, among them Big Minh's brother.

Nguyen Ngoc Tho, the junta's designated prime minister, championed the idea of wooing noncommunists away from the Viet Cong, and of competing with the NLF politically as well as militarily. He thought the first step in that direction was to bring together everyone in the south under a government of reconciliation. The junta asked that the Buddhists and students end their protests and find peaceful ways to take part in the society. The ultimate goal, according to the prime minister, was a "neutral government — not a government without an army, but one without foreign troops or bases and one whose neutrality in international affairs would incline towards the West." These high-minded goals were the exact opposite of what the United States wanted.

The United States had decided that the South Vietnamese should be working on an aggressive battlefield strategy to fight the north instead of spending time on political campaigns in the south. In December 1963 the Americans asked the junta to approve a proposal for bombing the north. Big Minh refused and also ignored American pleas to start new military campaigns in the countryside.

The American military leaders were furious with the junta, particularly after U.S. Embassy officials in Saigon discovered that junta members were promoting the idea of a neutral government without first discussing it with them.

The Viet Cong, however, moved quickly to openly support reconciliation. They proposed free elections throughout the south to choose representatives from all areas to form a coalition government that would include both the Viet Cong and the Saigon regime. Foreign leaders, especially French President Charles de Gaulle, were promoting just such an idea. But the United States did not want to hear this advice. Some American officials feared this was an elaborate conspiracy to aid the northern communists, and they let the South Vietnamese junta leaders know that they did not like the idea.

In January 1964 the junta was overthrown before it had a chance to test its ideas. Some historians say this was the

United States' best opportunity to make a face-saving exit, which would have avoided the loss of thousands of American lives and tens of thousands of Vietnamese lives.

Lobbying the President

When Lyndon Johnson became the thirty-sixth president of the United States, his overriding concerns were to eliminate official segregation of the races in America and to alleviate abject poverty. He proposed doing this through a set of programs he said would create a "Great Society." A former senator from Texas, Johnson was a self-made man who showed great compassion for Americans whose progress was blocked by poverty and prejudice. But as a wheeling and dealing politician, he could also be ruthless and cunning, without pity for his enemies. During his years as president those two sides were at war with each other.

The compassionate Lyndon Johnson was engrossed with his plans for opening up American society to the underprivileged, but Vietnam immediately demanded his attention. On November 26, 1963, just four days after Kennedy's assassination, Johnson wrote in an action memorandum that he reconfirmed America's policy to fight "the externally directed and supported Communist conspiracy" in South Vietnam. He pledged to withdraw 1,000 U.S. military advisers from the south by year's end and authorized clandestine spying operations against North Vietnam to be conducted by South Vietnam with U.S. assistance. Those spying operations set in motion America's direct involvement in fighting the Vietnam War.

Johnson believed that his first mission as president was

to hold the country together after the shock and anguish of Kennedy's assassination. One of Johnson's close friends, lawyer Clark Clifford, explained, "When you come in as president under those circumstances, so suddenly and so quickly, you want to keep the team together. You can't organize a team in a matter of days or weeks or even months. Also, it was very clear that after the assassination, President Kennedy's popularity grew all the time. . . . He had become a martyr president, and I think President Johnson felt that it was advisable to keep that team."

Keeping Kennedy's top advisers ensured that Johnson also kept the Vietnam War. McGeorge Bundy, the national security adviser, moved quickly to steer Johnson away from the dangerous trend toward neutralism in South Vietnam. He wrote the new president a convincing memorandum saying that neutralism would lead to a "rapid collapse of anti-Communist forces in South Vietnam, and a unification of the whole country on Communist terms. Neutrality in Thailand and increased influence for Hanoi and Peking. Collapse of the anti-communist position in Laos. Heavy pressure on . . . Malaysia. A shift towards neutrality in Japan and the Philippines. Blows to U.S. prestige in South Korea and Taiwan which would require compensating increases in American commitment." Bundy's message was a restatement of the domino theory, in which one country's fall would lead to another's fall until a whole string of nations had tumbled to communism.

Johnson never asked Bundy to explain how and why he had drawn such extreme conclusions in which a neutral or even communist South Vietnam would ruin America's position in Asia. The president did not ask Bundy to provide the facts behind his arguments or the history of Vietnam and the war. If Bundy had been a senator asking for support of some legislation or a Texan businessman asking for a favor, the president would have grilled him on the issue and on the advantages and disadvantages of his request. But many of Johnson's friends believed the president, who was from a modest background, was intimidated by Kennedy's intellectual advisers and deferred to them rather than demand they prove themselves. Bundy, for example, had been a dean of Harvard College, an impressive achievement, but he had no background either in Vietnam or the science of warfare.

On the other hand, Bundy knew how to play the game of politics. He reminded Johnson in that memo of the upcoming presidential election in November 1964. Certainly Johnson did not want to risk losing South Vietnam to the communists before the election. Bundy reminded Johnson of the tactics used in the 1950s by Republican senators who had smeared Democrats for "losing" China to the communists. Johnson accepted Bundy's recommendations and said he would stop any talk of neutralism in South Vietnam.

Another holdover from the Kennedy administration whom Johnson was especially reluctant to challenge was Secretary of Defense Robert S. McNamara. Formerly the head of Ford Motor Company, McNamara had been asked by Kennedy to take over the Defense Department because of his fame as a modern manager. McNamara was a whizz at numbers and statistics, at figuring out how to classify and solve problems. Considering all the managerial problems at the Pentagon, McNamara's appointment made sense. He seemed the ideal person to tackle the perpetual million-dollar cost overruns and find the most cost-effective ways to design and produce weapons.

But McNamara saw himself as more than an office manager. He wanted to wage war, not simply oversee production of hardware for war. Early on he had focused on Vietnam as the most complex foreign political situation the United States had faced since World War II. McNamara's strength as a manager proved to be his undoing as a political thinker. As his biographer, Paul Henderickson, has pointed out, McNamara concentrated on the "quantifiable — all the statistics and none of the meaning" during the buildup of American forces in Vietnam.

McNamara immediately became Johnson's most influential adviser on the war, pushing aside Secretary of State Dean Rusk, who normally would have defined America's political purpose in foreign affairs. Rusk, however, seemed willing to allow McNamara to take over the Vietnam portfolio.

McNamara set the narrow intellectual tone for the debate within Johnson's inner circle. He approached the war much as he had Ford Motor Company, focusing on the details of American intelligence reports and reducing complicated political events to one-sentence paragraphs. He was far removed from the blood and fatigue of the war in tropical Southeast Asia and did not have the background or instincts to convert data from the field into successful policy.

Will South Vietnam Hold?

By 1964 McNamara's subordinates began having second thoughts about what Vietnam truly meant for the United

States. They asked how that small Asian nation could be powerful enough to destroy America's reputation in Asia, much less lead a communist insurrection from the South China Sea up to Japan. As author David Halberstam wrote, McNamara's advisers were asking, "If the government in Saigon was weak and probably not viable [if it could not last] was it worthwhile to try and bolster it? Were we committing ourselves to something that did not exist [South Vietnam], and if so, wasn't it extremely dangerous?"

These aides never raised their doubts with McNamara; they knew he had no sympathy for such questions. But McNamara himself would highlight some of these points in the months ahead. Johnson considered McNamara his favorite "expert" on Vietnam and asked the secretary to go there and find out how the war was going. In December 1963 McNamara went on a three-day fact-finding mission to Vietnam, but in that time he heard only the same things he had read in reports back in Washington.

Even so, on his return he told Johnson that he found the new government "indecisive and drifting," and he said the communist guerrillas had made enormous strides since Diem's assassination less than two months earlier. McNamara said that the pattern of Viet Cong success had begun escalating earlier in the summer of 1963, but that the United States had been unaware of it because Diem had covered it up.

Now the junta under Big Minh had reversed Diem's habit of lying about defeats and was reporting accurately the Viet Cong's successes. (The American military command in Saigon had also failed to report earlier Viet Cong victories.) But the junta's honesty was unwelcome. The American military continued to suppress reports of the difficulties the

South Vietnamese army had in holding off the communists. McNamara wanted Johnson to believe that the Vietnam War could be won, at least in the south, and to doubt the junta leaders who suggested the contrary.

On the battlefields of the south, whether in the marshy Mekong delta, the Central Highlands, or up north near the demilitarized zone (DMZ) separating North and South Vietnam, McNamara's views were irrelevant. In the small villages, in the larger towns, and increasingly in the cities, the communists' strategy was working; politics was on their side. Vietnam was a political war, no matter how often McNamara insisted otherwise, and the Saigon government did not offer a strong, attractive political alternative to the Vietnamese communists.

For better or worse, the communists clearly understood why they were fighting and were able to convince others to join them. Their political success was demonstrated on the battlefield as well. An early example was a battle that came to be known as Ap Bac.

The town of Bac is in the delta south of Saigon. John Paul Vann, an American adviser, decided that a battle there would demonstrate that the South Vietnamese could win in a traditional direct engagement with the communist guerrillas. In this battle, fought early in 1963, the Viet Cong stood their ground under attack by the South Vietnamese army.

The Saigon army had all the technological advantages the United States could provide, including support from a modern air force that dropped napalm — a burning jellylike compound — armored personnel carriers (lightweight troop transport tanks), and modern helicopters to carry them to the battlefields.

The Vietnamese communists were outnumbered by the

Saigon forces and outgunned, with no modern equipment to speak of. Their sole advantage was determination. The South Vietnam forces could not claim that the guerrillas melted into the jungle, refusing to fight. At the start of the engagement the Viet Cong fought intelligently and courageously, while many of the South Vietnamese soldiers and some of their officers simply refused to fight. One could call their behavior cowardly, but much of the reason for their refusal to fight was political. The South Vietnamese believed they were fighting America's war in Vietnam, and they saw little reason to risk casualties to serve the foreigners' purposes.

But the Vietnamese communists believed they were fighting what their leaders called a "people's war." North Vietnam's military chief, General Vo Nguyen Giap, the hero of Dien Bien Phu, convinced his soldiers and the population that this was a war where "the whole people, the whole country fights the aggressors with the people's armed forces as the hard core." The communists were not fighting for foreign advisers, they were fighting for General Giap.

The propaganda about the "people's war" was successful and resulted in nearly complete mobilization. Communists in the north and south were required to contribute to the war effort: farmers were asked to provide food, young children were drafted to place booby traps. Families had to give up sons, and even daughters, to the communist armed forces, which always needed more soldiers to replace those fallen in battle. In the communist literature, these harsh demands were painted in glorious detail: "Combining armed with political struggle, building combat villages everywhere, fighting both in the countryside and the towns, in the plains and in the mountains, using rudimentary weapons, traps and modern arms captured from the enemy, the population and the liberation armed forces set up a vast net which paralyzed the giant U.S.-puppet military [the South Vietnamese army]."

These were the soldiers who faced down the South Vietnamese and their American advisers at the battle of Ap Bac with cunning and courage. As author Neil Sheehan wrote in *A Bright Shining Lie*, "The 350 guerrillas had stood their ground and humbled a modern army four times their number equipped with armor and artillery and supported by helicopters and fighter bombers." The battle was over within twenty-four hours, and the Viet Cong won a full victory.

The Vietnamese communists immediately declared the battle of Ap Bac a watershed in the war. They wrote: "At Ap Bac . . . helicopters and amphibious tanks — proved quite vulnerable. After Ap Bac, 1963 was marked with severe set-backs for the [Saigon] army; the victories of the [communist] forces greatly helped the population to wage a tenacious and victorious struggle against . . . strategic hamlets." The communists used this victory to launch an "emulation drive," asking other soldiers to copy the courage of those who had defended Ap Bac.

This was the situation the junta inherited after overthrowing Diem. Officers in the Saigon armed forces were trained to avoid fighting, to avoid casualties, and to follow the orders of their political patrons. Big Minh and the other junta members said they wanted to reform the military, and during McNamara's visit in December 1963 they discussed their problems openly. McNamara's response was to blame

Minh and the junta for the problems left over from Diem's regime.

The Return of the Overlords

A few weeks after McNamara's visit, in January 1964, a young field commander named General Nguyen Khanh overthrew the junta. Johnson's top advisers had decided that the United States needed to increase its military role in Vietnam, and some American officials apparently encouraged the coup, hoping Khanh would allow America's involvement to escalate. Khanh's own American adviser was deeply involved in the coup, radioing reports to the U.S. Embassy in Saigon asking for assurances that the United States did not object to Khanh's plans. Only a few months after the coup against Diem, an American was helping a rebellious officer overthrow the Saigon government, this time the junta of Big Minh.

This time the American president did not agonize over the moral or political questions posed by a coup. Johnson simply said this should be the last coup; he wanted "no more of this coup shit." A spokesman at the U.S. Embassy was more circumspect. He said the coup was really a "change in the Chairmanship and composition of the Military Revolutionary Council." But this "change" was made with tanks and soldiers, top officials were arrested and threatened with execution, and the action had all the hallmarks of a coup.

One of the first messages Khanh sent to Washington was a vow that he would "rely heavily" on the American ambassador for advice, which was exactly what the U.S. government wanted. Big Minh had disappointed the Americans by refusing to allow the bombing of the north and by protecting himself from their pressure to take control of the war. Khanh did not object to being told how to wage war and run the government.

Khanh opened the door to a flood of new American advisers: the number rose from 16,300 to 23,300 in nine months. All over the country tall American military men with big American smiles were seen beside their generally smaller Vietnamese counterparts, cast in the all too familiar role of listening to foreigners tell them how to run their country. Soon the Vietnamese started calling the Americans *co van vi dai*, a term used for Chinese overlords centuries earlier.

The American overlords were as irritating to the Vietnamese as the Chinese had been. A respected Saigon journalist wrote, "With a conviction of their superiority, the Americans are obsessively concerned about 'advising' the Vietnamese. . . . They seem to believe that anyone could be an adviser of some sort provided he be an American. Thus there are Americans who hardly know anything about Vietnam and counterinsurgency advising Vietnamese officials on pacification, advisers who have no qualifications in refugee matters 'advising' Vietnamese social workers, Americans who have no solid knowledge of Vietnamese administrative problems 'advising' local administrators, and so on."

While the American military "advisers" died fighting, as often as not their South Vietnamese comrades ducked out of the battle. The Americans wondered why the South Vietnamese criticized them for trampling on their national pride but did not fight for their nation themselves. And the Vietnamese resented the foreign overlords. This relationship of mutual resentment between the American GIs and their South Vietnamese allies remained the same throughout the war.

Khanh's reward for welcoming American advisers in large numbers was active U.S. protection against any stirrings of a coup against him, for the first year at least. President Johnson opened up the American treasury to pay for Khanh's war. He cabled Ambassador Lodge in Saigon: "In our effort to help the Vietnamese to help themselves, we must not let any arbitrary limits on budget, or manpower, or procedures stand in our way. You must have whatever you need to help the Vietnamese do the job, and I assure you that I will act at once to eliminate obstacles or restraints wherever they may appear." Johnson's open-ended spending to win the Vietnam War brought about the beginning of an American economic recession.

Although Khanh was saying yes to American requests, his army continued to say no to aggressive combat. As a result, the communists easily won victory after victory in the south. No matter what Khanh said to Washington, his army changed little; the soldiers did not accept American views about how to win a war, and they fought their own way on their own terms.

In the spring of 1964 Secretary of Defense McNamara made another trip to South Vietnam to bolster support for Khanh. Although he traveled throughout the country, smiling for the camera alongside the diminutive Khanh, McNamara could smell defeat in the air. He reported back to President Johnson: "The situation has unquestionably been growing worse . . . in the last 90 days the weakening of the government's position has been particularly noticeable." He spelled out the evidence: "Large groups of the population are now showing signs of apathy and indifference. . . . The [South Vietnamese army] and paramilitary desertion rates are high and increasing. . . . Draft dodging is high while the Viet Cong are recruiting energetically and effectively."

Something had to be done. McNamara was prepared to argue that America had to go to war.

In the Cool of the Office

One by one, President Johnson's advisers lobbied him to send American ground forces and warplanes to Vietnam. They believed that if the United States did not fight the war and win it, the South Vietnamese would fight it and lose, dragging down the United States and most of the free world.

Johnson's advisers failed to see the third option of continuing to provide South Vietnam with financial assistance but allowing them to win or lose on their own. Choosing this option would have meant recognizing that Johnson's advisers, particularly McNamara, had misjudged the nature of the war. The third option would have made it clear that the war was a dispute between the Vietnamese people that was supported by outside powers. It would have been far more difficult to justify sending America's youth to a far-away jungle war they knew so little about. And McNamara would have had to be honest about the slim chances any Saigon government had of surviving on its own.

A British officer who had fought in and lost an earlier war in the Southeast Asian jungles warned of the dangers of following the orders and policies of commanders back home. These men, he wrote, had "an academic bureaucratic outlook, formed in the cool of an office or the comfort of the road, scarcely ever in the rubber jungle with its storms and claustrophobic oppressiveness." Their wrong-headed orders, he said, were based on "little or no realism in the sense of appreciating facts and conditions as they really were." Such attitudes were reflected in the memoranda written over the next several months by Americans in the "cool of an office."

The top military man in the United States was the chairman of the Joint Chiefs of Staff, General Maxwell Taylor. In a memo to McNamara he wrote: "The US must be prepared to put aside many of the self-imposed restrictions which limit our efforts, and to undertake bolder actions which may embody greater risks."

Taylor said America's reputation for "durability, resolution and trustworthiness" was at stake. If the United States failed, the repercussions would be felt throughout Asia and "in Africa and in Latin America." He went on to detail the "self-imposed" restrictions he wanted to do away with, such as keeping the war inside the boundaries of South Vietnam, preventing U.S. soldiers from fighting in combat, and limiting Americans to advisory roles. The general did not mention that these were normal restrictions for a nation not officially at war. Instead he recommended starting a bombing campaign in North Vietnam and sending U.S. combat troops into battle in the south. These were acts of war, which by the law of the United States could not be done without an official declaration of war by Congress against the Hanoi government. Taylor did not recommend such a declaration.

McNamara answered Taylor in a confidential memo in

March 1964, written after his brief tour of South Vietnam with Khanh. He agreed that the world was watching how the United States was handling this situation, and he said that "the stakes are high." However, McNamara disagreed that an immediate escalation was necessary. McNamara wanted to build up the South Vietnamese police and armed forces, improve U.S. air support and air reconnaissance (information gathering), and counteract the communist guerrilla successes with a southern version of guerrilla warfare.

After more memos and conversations that spring, President Johnson asked that plans be drawn up for a bombing of the north if it became necessary. This was the first step toward widening the war. In May the president's advisers drew up another secret plan — again, just in case it was needed. When passed into law by Congress, this resolution would give the president war powers, or the legal right to wage war, without actually declaring war.

The bombing plan and the draft legislation empowering the president to enact it were in place. All that was missing was the excuse to put these secret plans into action.

The Long Summer of 1964

In June 1964, General William C. Westmoreland replaced General Harkins as head of America's military mission in Vietnam. After failing to convince Kennedy to oppose the overthrow of Diem, Harkins had become convinced that the South Vietnamese could win the war. Harkins had not only failed in his job, he had confused that failure with success. At a farewell dinner in Saigon, he said, "I leave Vietnam convinced that the tide is going to turn soon."

Westmoreland understood that Harkins was mistaken

in his optimism and was determined to do better. He launched a scheme called *hop tap*, a Vietnamese term for cooperation, aimed at convincing the peasants to support Saigon rather than the Viet Cong. It was a variation of an old French strategy that had failed during the earlier Indochina War.

Another change in the American presence in South Vietnam was the resignation of Henry Cabot Lodge to run for the Republican presidential nomination. Johnson appointed General Taylor, the head of the Joint Chiefs, to replace him, a move that was intended to prevent any Republican adversary from accusing him of being "soft" or "weak" against the Vietnamese communists.

Johnson was preparing his Vietnam policy very much with the presidential election in mind. He was haunted by the memories of the fifties, when politicians and diplomats were ruined by accusations of being "soft" on China and allowing the communists to win that country. Johnson planned to paint the American effort in Vietnam with strong, patriotic colors. He also wanted the war to be seen as Kennedy's war. "I think President Kennedy felt very strongly that we should not permit Southeast Asia to fall into the hands of the communists," Johnson said.

But the South Vietnamese were not acting according to Johnson's script. Students were protesting again in Saigon, and the United States was spending about $2 million a day to prop up a government that Ambassador Taylor predicted had no more than a "fifty to fifty chance of lasting out the year."

Then, in the middle of the presidential election campaign that summer, trouble broke out in the Gulf of Tonkin, off the coast of North Vietnam. Some North Vietnamese boats attacked a large American ship in a clash that came on as suddenly as a summer storm. But like a storm that ends a period of stifling heat, this incident was the climax of weeks of intrigue and tension that had to break.

The conflict originated when Johnson approved a request by the intelligence-gathering arm of the U.S. military to engage in top-secret operations in the waters off North Vietnam to determine whether the North Vietnamese could protect their coasts and their skies from American jet bombers. The intelligence operation was to be a cat-and-mouse game. The U.S. officers would send South Vietnamese naval commando units to attack the North Vietnamese bases, provoking a response; farther out in the gulf, large American naval ships would measure the North Vietnamese reaction. But what was meant to be a "test in case of war" became the trigger that brought the United States into the war.

At the end of July the South Vietnamese commando units began their attack. Their mission was especially difficult because the Gulf of Tonkin is regularly covered by fog and mist, and its seas are choppy and dangerous to navigate. The South Vietnamese sprayed machine gun fire from their small boats at North Vietnamese bases and fled quickly into the protective cover of fog, while the U.S. naval ships monitored the attack and sent the sensitive information straight to Washington.

Immediately the North Vietnamese protested the attack as well as the presence of American destroyers so close to their shore. In a telegram to the International Control Commission, an agency established by the 1954 Geneva Conference, the Hanoi government protested that "on 30 July the

Americans and their henchmen in South Vietnam sent two warships to bombard [two North Vietnamese islands]. . . . The Vietnam People's Army strongly protests the above-mentioned bombardments of these two islands by the warship of the Americans and their henchmen . . . and urges the Americans and the southern administration to stop immediately their extremely dangerous and provocative acts."

The United States responded that its ships were ten miles out at sea, which is considered within international waters, where any ship has a right to travel. And the Americans stated that the destroyer, the *Maddox*, would stay where it was. The North Vietnamese, however, did not accept the claim that international waters began ten miles off their coast. On the morning of August 2, dozens of small Vietnamese fishing boats called junks surrounded the *Maddox*. To avoid a fight the captain of the destroyer moved away from the junks, even though his superiors had told him to stay put and continue the intelligence mission. Around noon three North Vietnamese patrol boats attacked the ship; within twenty minutes the *Maddox* had crippled two of the boats and had sunk the third. The *Maddox* itself was hardly scratched, and no American was injured.

President Johnson telephoned Soviet leader Nikita Khrushchev on the "hot line" (the telephone reserved for emergencies arising between the two superpowers) to assure him that the United States was not trying to widen the war in Vietnam. He also sent a diplomatic note to Hanoi protesting the North Vietnamese attack. The president contended that the communists had no right to fire on American ships on the "high seas" (international waters). Johnson's aides went even further. They pulled out the sample law McGeorge

Bundy had written to expand the president's war powers and got it ready for Congress to act on.

All U.S. combat troops in Southeast Asia were placed on alert, and the navy dispatched another aircraft carrier to the South China Sea in case orders were given for American jets to bomb targets in the north, specifically oil depots. As one expert said, the carriers were used to "bait" the communists, to dare them to attack.

The next morning the South Vietnamese commandos again fired from their boats at North Vietnamese bases. This time, however, the captain of the *Maddox* wanted no part in a South Vietnamese attack and radioed his commanders for permission to retreat from the scene. Just after that an intelligence officer aboard the *Maddox* heard on the radio what sounded like North Vietnamese orders to attack the ship. The captain radioed a warning to Washington and put the ship on a zigzag course to avoid torpedoes from the North Vietnamese boats. Some odd dots on the *Maddox*'s radar screens were interpreted as torpedoes, which the captain reported to Washington as an attack on his ship. Two U.S. carriers waiting nearby sent fighter jets to defend the *Maddox*, but one of the pilots returning from the mission said no attack had occurred. No American ship had been hit, and there was no sign that a single torpedo had exploded.

The radar findings could easily have been caused by stormy weather or mechanical problems. There was no other evidence of an attack by the North Vietnamese. And after a forty-minute search, the pilots sent to protect the *Maddox* had not found any North Vietnamese patrol boats.

In Washington, however, Johnson and his aides accepted the first report of an attack, and the president immediately ordered a retaliation. The United States was poised to bomb North Vietnam, as Taylor had counseled months before. President Johnson told several senators and congressmen that he would ask the full Congress to pass a resolution already prepared by his aides, giving him full power to respond to the North Vietnamese. He then asked McNamara for reports verifying the attack.

The *Maddox*'s captain and crew were in the dark about what had occurred. From eight in the evening to midnight the ship had seemed to be under attack, but the captain said the "entire action leaves many doubts." He hoped to clear up the matter the next day with a thorough search in daylight.

President Johnson did not wait for the captain's final report. In a televised address he told the American people that the United States had launched its first bombing mission over North Vietnamese territory. Consciously or not, the president's aides and his military chiefs had been working toward this goal all that year.

The Tonkin Gulf Resolution

Immediately American jets flew sixty-four sorties, or bombing missions, against North Vietnamese patrol boat bases and an oil depot. President Johnson and his advisers claimed that these missions were in retaliation for a second attack against the American ships, which meant they were simply ignoring the later reports that doubted an attack had ever taken place.

The first of these bombing raids proved that an air war would be costly. Two American airplanes were shot down, and one pilot was taken prisoner after parachuting to safety. The first prisoner in America's undeclared war against

Hanoi, he was locked up in a dingy local jail. Among his first visitors was Pham Van Dong, one of the top leaders of the North Vietnamese government.

In Washington, President Johnson portrayed the Tonkin Gulf incident simply as a North Vietnamese attack against a U.S. naval vessel. He and his advisers never told the public or Congress that the *Maddox* was on an intelligence mission, that South Vietnamese commandos had provoked the first clash with the North Vietnamese, that the South Vietnamese had raided the coast a second time, or that the *Maddox* had been a decoy during that raid. And Congress was certainly not aware that no solid evidence existed of a second North Vietnamese attack.

The Johnson administration presented Congress with a resolution that would allow the bombing of the north to continue. Patterned after Bundy's secret draft resolution written in May, it began with the White House version of the Tonkin Gulf events, presented its case against the north, and then authorized "the President, as Commander in Chief, to take all necessary measures to repel any armed attack against the forces of the United States and to prevent further aggression." The resolution also said that Southeast Asia was "vital" to America's national interest and to world peace and that therefore the president should be allowed "to take all necessary steps, including the use of armed forces" to assist certain countries in the region, including South Vietnam, that ask for "defense of its freedom." There was no time limit on the resolution; Congress was being asked to give the president unlimited war powers for an unlimited war. In addition, Johnson was asking for these extraordinary powers without actually declaring war on North Vietnam.

During the debate on the resolution, one maverick

member of Congress, Senator Wayne Morse of Oregon, asked McNamara if the *Maddox* had been part of an intelligence mission, if this whole incident hadn't been a setup to push the United States into war. Morse had received a tip from a military source that the *Maddox* indeed was on a provocative intelligence mission.

The defense secretary denied that the South Vietnamese had been working with the *Maddox*, even though he knew better. Senator Morse lost the argument, and the Senate approved the resolution by a vote of forty-two in favor, two opposed. The law, dated August 7, 1964, became known as the Tonkin Gulf Resolution.

Senator Ernest Gruening of Alaska, who joined Morse in opposing the resolution, came to the point in explaining his vote: "All Vietnam is not worth the life of a single American boy." Gruening did not believe that Vietnam was the first line of defense against the collapse of the free world. He felt that this theory was unproven and far-fetched. When he asked why a single American life should be lost in this civil war between the Vietnamese, no one in the debate answered him. Senator Morse told his Senate colleagues they would all live to regret their votes.

Among the first to criticize America's action in the Gulf of Tonkin was Soviet leader Khrushchev. He wrote to Johnson asking why American warships had been in the gulf other than "as a challenge to the states whose shores are washed by that Gulf" (North Vietnam and communist China).

Khrushchev continued, "With all frankness I must say that if these actions of American warships and air force pursue the aim of strengthening somehow the position of the

corrupt and rotten South Vietnamese regime which exists
— and this is no secret to anyone — only because of the
foreign support, then such actions will not achieve the given
aim. But to increase the danger of a serious military conflict
— they can. . . . I would like to hope that on your part there
will be shown necessary composure and restraint."

Johnson did not budge an inch. In his reply to Khrushchev he overstated his case: "I think you can understand that
the second deliberate attack — on which there is complete
and incontrovertible evidence — could not be allowed to
pass without reply."

A few days later, however, the president told one of his
aides what he really thought about that second attack.
"Hell," he said, "those dumb stupid sailors were just shooting at flying fish." Johnson was not going to admit that he
knew the evidence of a second attack was flimsy at best. The
point was to win the permission of Congress to go to war
without declaring war. And the Tonkin Gulf Resolution
accomplished that purpose.

Khrushchev was not the only leader who feared that the
United States was about to embark on a major war. Diplomats and leaders in the noncommunist as well as the communist world openly asked what would come of America's
direct participation in Vietnam. Why, they wondered, was
the United States investing its money and prestige in a war
the French had already lost and that Saigon was clearly losing? How would the rest of the world be affected if the
superpower of the West went to war? Would the Soviet
Union or China send its soldiers to fight alongside the North
Vietnamese army?

U Thant, who as secretary general of the United

Nations was the world leader directly charged with trying to avoid war, attempted to organize face-to-face talks between Hanoi and Washington. Khrushchev agreed to help bring the North Vietnamese to the negotiating table. Even though Khrushchev was overthrown by hard-liners that October, the North Vietnamese agreed in February 1965 to meet with the Americans.

But the U.S. government absolutely refused to talk to the North Vietnamese. Angry and frustrated that he could not prevent what he foresaw as an explosive, bloody war, U Thant broke all the diplomatic rules of the United Nations and appealed publicly to the American people, warning them not to become entangled in Vietnam.

He said, "I am sure the great American people, if only they knew the true facts and background to the development in South Viet-Nam, will agree with me that further bloodshed is unnecessary. And that political and diplomatic methods of discussions and negotiations alone can create conditions which will enable the United States to withdraw gracefully from that part of the world. As you know, in times of war and of hostilities the first casualty is the truth."

U Thant was saying that America's leaders were liars. This, of course, made Johnson and his advisers furious, particularly because of the uncanny timing of U Thant's speech. He spoke in February 1965, the time the United States had secretly decided would be the end of negotiations; America was preparing to send in combat troops.

From Tonkin to Da Nang

One of the American pilots sent on that first air raid over North Vietnam remembered his surprise and anguish when told that the air strikes were reprisals for the previous night's attacks on a U.S. destroyer in the Gulf of Tonkin. The pilot wrote, "I felt like I had been doused with ice water. How do I get in touch with the President? He's going off half-cocked." The pilot knew the destroyer had not been attacked, but he obeyed orders, was later captured, and spent seven years in a North Vietnamese prison.

With the Tonkin Gulf Resolution passed into law, Johnson hit the campaign trail, saying he would not be easy on either our ally or our enemy in Vietnam. In September he promised, "I have not thought we were ready for American boys to do the fighting for Asian boys. What I have been trying to do, with the situation that I found, was to get the boys in Vietnam to do their own fighting with our advice and our equipment."

In October Johnson made a firmer commitment not to send U.S. troops into battle: "We are not about to send American boys away from home to do what Asian boys ought to be doing for themselves."

When American voters went to the polls a few weeks later, they believed they were being offered a real choice between war and peace. The Republican candidate, Senator Barry Goldwater of Arizona, had said he was in favor of an air offensive against the north. Though Johnson had made one "retaliatory raid" against the north, he was promising peace in the long term. Goldwater tried to portray Johnson's policy as "appeasement" and asked instead for a U.S. victory, even if it had to be achieved with "low-yield atomic weapons." That proposal, made twice, was a boon to the Democrats; they televised a political advertisement showing a young child pulling petals off a flower, followed by an atomic explosion.

Secretly, however, the Johnson administration had also considered dropping nuclear weapons, but only if Chinese troops joined in the fighting alongside the North Vietnamese forces. By this time the Johnson inner circle considered an air war against the north and the introduction of U.S. troops necessary steps to stop the communist momentum. This was as serious an escalation of the American role as that proposed by Goldwater.

These discussions and decisions were hidden from the public. Johnson won the election in November 1964 with the largest margin in American history and helped his fellow Democrats win strong majorities in the House of Representatives and the Senate. Johnson could now lead the United States to peace in Vietnam, as he had promised, or to war, as he had been planning.

Before he could choose either path, events in Saigon again caught the president by surprise. During the American presidential campaign, the people of South Vietnam had been openly plotting to get rid of General Khanh; they believed he had become a corrupt tyrant, imposing new censorship laws and declaring martial law without improving the government or the army, much less figuring out a way to win the war. Diem's old rivals were aiming at Khanh. Buddhist monks and students with placards took to the streets in a march of some 25,000 citizens. And secretly a group of disgruntled military officers decided this was a good moment for another coup d'état.

They tried twice. On September 2 and again on September 11, two different groups of senior officers launched coups. Each time the U.S. government stepped in to save the fragile Saigon regime (and Johnson's election prospects). On

September 11 U.S. military advisers persuaded the South Vietnamese officers to abort their coup, while the radio station Voice of America broadcast appeals to the public to save the regime.

Even so, there was nothing resembling peace in the streets of Saigon. In continuing demonstrations, Catholics and Buddhists, students and gangsters fought against the government and each other. Windows were smashed, bullets were fired in anger, and several demonstrators were killed. Various political groups tried to win over the students. Khanh had tried to deflect criticism by blaming the French government for promoting a peaceful end to the war and neutrality. He told the students to demonstrate against the French Embassy in Saigon. They refused, saying, "The French aren't even here. How can we blame our problems on them?"

Several communist front groups in Saigon encouraged the students to continue pressuring Khanh and to overthrow his government. But the students were not sure that it was a good idea to overthrow yet another general. "We want a role in building our nation rather than just overthrowing governments," they said.

In the autumn of 1964 such innocence was still possible in the south. The students came up with a project charged with idealism; they would move out of Saigon and help the rural poor who had become the true victims of the war. They left by the thousands and even founded their own newspaper called *Len Duong*, or "Hit the Road."

The students' timing could not have been worse for the American and South Vietnamese governments. The plans they were drawing up would prohibit any able-bodied man from going off to the villages as a social worker; all would be needed as soldiers. And those villages and rice fields would soon become too dangerous for the young women.

The idea encapsulated in the student newspaper name *Len Duong* was soon replaced with the slogan *Xuong Duong*, or "March Down the Road," which encouraged demonstrations against the Saigon government's war policies. The middle ground of idealism was disappearing. Young men either joined the army, bribed their way out of the draft, or fled the country. As one young southerner pondered his future, he said: "I was born in 1946, just as the first Indochina War was getting started. My father died fighting with the Viet Minh. I don't know how. The war has been going all my life and there is no end in sight. The first draft call for young men born in 1946 has gone out, and in September I'll certainly be drafted. I was born into a war, I have always lived in a war, and perhaps next year I'll finally die in it." Although he was born into war and might die in it, he neither understood or accepted it; that attitude was pervasive in South Vietnam.

In November 1964 Ambassador Taylor wrote a report for Johnson on the south's morale problem. "We sense the mounting feeling of war weariness and hopelessness which pervade South Viet-Nam," he wrote. "There is no national tendency towards team play or mutual loyalty to be found among many of the leaders and groups within South Viet-Nam." Taylor's remedy for this was a bombing campaign against North Vietnam, which could offer the Saigon government the "hope of ending the insurgency in some finite time."

But within this same report Taylor contradicted his

view that the morale problem was a cultural phenomenon. Like American military advisers before him, Taylor praised the Viet Cong's "amazing ability to maintain morale."

The Viet Cong came from the same culture as the South Vietnamese soldiers, and Taylor was not the first American to wonder what accounted for the difference. "The ability of the Viet-Cong continuously to rebuild their units and to make good their losses is one of the mysteries of this guerrilla war," he wrote. "We are aware of the recruiting methods by which local boys are induced or compelled to join the Viet-Cong ranks. . . . We still find no plausible explanation of the continued strength of the Viet-Cong."

Taylor never did understand the mystery, as he called it, of why the soldiers of the South Vietnamese government were less committed to fight than the Viet Cong. American policy refused to allow him or anyone else to ask the questions that would solve the mystery. The answer was that the war was a political conflict between groups of the Vietnamese. The communists felt strongly about their reasons for fighting, while the southerners felt they had little say over their country's destiny — that seemed to be in the hands of the Americans. It was ironic that the Viet Cong soldiers earned about a dollar a month, while the privates of the South Vietnamese army earned twenty times that amount, were better equipped and fed, yet were deserting at an alarming rate. The ambassador ended his report by stating flatly, "We are playing a losing game in South Vietnam."

Taylor's concern was to avoid the consequences he thought would result from a defeat in Vietnam. He argued that bombing the north would prevent more arms, supplies, and soldiers from getting to the south because the Viet

Cong would be cut off from their sources. And if Hanoi realized the bombing was in retaliation for communist attacks on Americans, the north would be weakened. Taylor concluded that such a campaign would also bolster the faltering regime in Saigon.

But before Taylor's proposals could be implemented, that regime exploded. In December 1964 a group of South Vietnamese officers known as the Young Turks arrested civilian officials and political leaders who refused to obey them and got rid of a civilian legislative body. They did not overthrow Khanh; they simply removed bothersome civilians and politicians. Khanh himself called a news conference to announce the changes and the arrests.

Ambassador Taylor was furious. He called a meeting with the Young Turks, during which he could barely control his temper. "I told you all clearly at General Westmoreland's dinner we Americans are tired of coups. Apparently I wasted my words. . . . Now you have made a real mess. We cannot carry you forever if you do things like this."

A South Vietnamese admiral spoke up after several others had responded. "It seems that we are being treated as though we were guilty," he said. "What we did was good and we did it only for the good of the country."

Taylor did not give up. He said the United States wanted more civilian rule, not less, and asked why these officers had not warned him of their plans. "Why don't you tell your friends before you act?"

The ambassador telephoned Khanh and told him to leave the country. But Khanh was not about to give up. He tape-recorded the conversation, including Taylor's orders. He then warned the South Vietnamese people about "foreign" intervention in Vietnamese affairs, and by January 1965 protestors in the streets of Saigon were demanding that Taylor resign as ambassador. In Hue students broke into the library of the United States Information Service and tore it apart. Saigon was alive with rumors of a real coup, and Khanh's government was in shambles. In February Khanh resigned in the midst of an attempted coup.

The Viet Cong made steady gains in the countryside and started attacking the growing number of U.S. installations in South Vietnam as the Americans became more visible obstacles. In November they attacked an American air base at Bien Hoa and killed four Americans. On Christmas Eve they attacked a barracks in Saigon, killing two more Americans.

President Johnson considered retaliatory bombing strikes on the north after each of these attacks but decided against them. He reasoned that the Saigon regime was too weak to profit from such attacks and that the air strikes would be of greatest benefit if they were coordinated with a strong South Vietnamese army attack on the Viet Cong once they were stranded without resupplies from the north.

As the demonstrations and trouble continued in Saigon, Ambassador Taylor's messages to Washington became more and more urgent. "To take no positive action now is to accept defeat in the fairly near future," he cabled. Taylor's warning was underlined by a memorandum to the president from McNamara and Bundy, saying that they, too, were "pretty well convinced that our current policy can lead only to disastrous defeat."

Bundy said they believed that "the [South] Vietnamese know just as we do that the Viet Cong are gaining in the countryside." He said the Saigon regime also felt that the United States was not exercising its "enormous power" — presumably its full military force — and did not believe that the United States had a "firm and active" policy. Bundy said, "The time has come for harder choices."

That memo was written on January 27, 1965, and on February 6 the Viet Cong attacked a U.S. army barracks at Pleiku and a nearby helicopter base. Nine Americans were killed in this attack.

This time Johnson struck back by ordering an air strike campaign called Flaming Dart against the north. Johnson told his advisers: "We have kept our gun over the mantel and our shells in the cupboard for a long time now. And what was the result? They are killing our men while they sleep in the night. I can't ask our American soldiers out there to continue to fight with one hand tied behind their backs."

Others pointed out, however, that American soldiers were not supposed to be fighting at all in Vietnam, only advising. Their weapons were to be used only to defend themselves. But Johnson wanted the American public to accept his Texan image of Americans caught by outlaws in the dead of night. He had gone to great lengths earlier to prove that the north was a sovereign nation that was breaking international law by sending its soldiers into South Vietnam. (International law did not support this logic, since Vietnam was considered a divided nation at war, but if North Vietnam *was* a "sovereign" nation, Johnson had no right to attack it without declaring war.)

Soon after Flaming Dart got under way, it was replaced by a larger campaign named Rolling Thunder, which had been planned far in advance. Bundy's explanation for this escalation of military action was that "Pleikus are like streetcars"; in other words, you catch the first one that comes by. The Viet Cong attack on Pleiku became America's excuse for implementing the policy Bundy and McNamara had favored all along.

McNamara wanted the United States to wage a sophisticated technological war that would inflict the greatest possible physical damage on North Vietnam while putting the fewest number of American lives at risk. America's greatest advantage over Vietnam was its technological prowess, the muscle Bundy wanted Johnson to use.

In such a war American airmen would still be at risk, and the question of their safety provided the opening for further escalation in the form of U.S. combat troops. General Westmoreland, the American military chief in South Vietnam, requested that two marine battalions be sent to protect the U.S. air base at Da Nang, from which the air war was to be launched against the north. The marines were not to be considered advisers. He wanted them to actively patrol and secure the bases and the surrounding area and to search for and engage the enemy.

In Washington Westmoreland's request was approved with little debate. Only Ambassador Taylor in Saigon warned that after sending these two battalions it would be "very difficult to hold [the] line" at sending other troops.

The Rolling Thunder air campaign began on March 2, 1965, when American bombers hit an ammunition depot in the north. On March 8, two marine battalions came ashore at Da Nang prepared to meet enemy fire. Instead they were welcomed by the mayor of the city and a delegation of young women who threw garlands around the necks of the soldiers.

The next day President Johnson made the controversial decision to authorize the use of napalm against North Vietnam. By the end of April the United States had flown 3,600 sorties against the north.

The United States had begun what would be the longest war in its history.

5

AT WAR

From the beginning, a small but vocal minority of Americans had doubts about the fighting in Vietnam. Young men publicly burned their draft cards, and in Vietnam even the most loyal soldiers raised the basic question, Why are we fighting in Vietnam? Because the United States went to war in Vietnam without a popular consensus or even active support, there was widespread confusion and dissent. What bothered many Americans was the roundabout way that the United States had become involved in this war. The different pieces of the puzzle somehow never fit together and never were satisfactorily explained.

As early as February 26, 1965, the poet Thomas Merton, a Catholic monk who lived in a cloistered monastery in the back hills of Kentucky, wrote a troubled letter about the war: "This Vietnam thing is sickening and just about as stupid as one would imagine possible, but I have an odd feeling that it is not going to get any more intelligent as time goes on. This country seems to be bent on giving everyone for all time a clear lesson in how to miss all one's opportunities to make a good use of power."

The division of opinion in the United States reflected the complications of the war. In the north the communist government had the communist world's support against what it saw as an American attempt to divide their country and deny them the victory they had won from France in 1954. In the south the lines were more blurred. The Viet Cong, known officially as the National Liberation Front, was relatively new and, although dependent on the communists of the north, included many noncommunists. At the beginning of Johnson's war in Vietnam the Viet Cong forces were still poorly armed peasants compared to the American troops and the equipment landing on Vietnam's beaches and flying into the new, modern bases. The people of South Vietnam were tolerant of, and often loyal to, the Viet Cong, who controlled much of the countryside and lived like the peasants in thatched houses or in far worse conditions in the hot, humid jungles where a hammock was home.

The Saigon government was, as ever, embroiled in power politics. Military officers continued to try to outmaneuver the Buddhists, the students, and the Americans. The United States spent enormous sums of money keeping the government afloat and putting the American army in place in the south. In the end the money and the suffocating American presence worked against the United States' aims for the south. The United States was undeniably calling the shots, even though the South Vietnamese leaders, behaving like spoiled children, routinely tried to circumvent American dictates. When the Saigon government did not like U.S. orders, it ignored them.

American soldiers walking into this morass were astonished. The country itself was a mystery. Saigon had the air of a sophisticated city; the countryside seemed part of a time long past. Which side of this warring country was for freedom, which was for evil? War normally answers such questions in the heat of battle. Freedom is your buddy, and evil is the guy trying to kill you. In Vietnam that formula failed. The GIs' buddies were supposed to be the soldiers of Saigon's army, but they routinely showed resentment of the American presence. Perhaps they saw the GIs as a blow to their pride. At the same time they let the Americans take over their fighting without demonstrating enthusiasm for the war or for helping their ally.

The citizens of South Vietnam were even more ambivalent; their loyalties were divided between the Saigon government and the Viet Cong; rarely did they show any gratitude to the American GI who was risking his life to save them.

The American community in Vietnam also included diplomats and journalists, few of whom properly understood the country or the war. The diplomats served with the same loyalty as the GIs, but with a different field of vision. They saw the war as part of the global struggle between the free world and communism. In their view, Hanoi was trying to force communism on the south and in the process aid all communists in defeating the free world.

Journalists covering the war were less convinced by abstract geopolitical theories. When these reporters found little that resembled freedom in the south, a persuasive minority began writing about America's heavy-handed presence and the fragmented loyalties and fears of the southerners themselves. Since the United States had not officially declared war, the American press was not censored by the government. Most American journalists were sympathetic to their country's side of the story, but in war Johnson wanted nothing less than one hundred percent loyalty. He grew angry when even a few influential reporters revealed aspects of the war he would have preferred to keep hidden.

As these bits of truth ricocheted back home, Americans began expressing doubts. President Johnson was trying to wage this war with a minimum of American casualties, relying on modern weaponry rather than on foot soldiers; later the strategy was known as a "war by proxy." The United States dropped a record number of bombs on Vietnam and used napalm, the defoliant known as Agent Orange, and other controversial means to devastate the enemy without getting hurt themselves. Scientists and other professionals decried this strategy, saying that the civilians of Vietnam and their environment — tropical forests and paddy fields — became the victims in the war.

On the other hand, some military experts argued loudly that the U.S. armed forces were not being allowed to destroy enough of Vietnam to win the war. They complained that American GIs were fighting "with one hand tied behind their backs" because of restrictions on bombing North Vietnam, and indeed on how much of Vietnam could be considered part of the battlefield. These were the questions soldiers asked when they were sent to Vietnam. The methods for fighting the war were baffling and, many believed, inappropriate.

This was the emotional and political backdrop of President Johnson's war in Vietnam. The confusion and raw feelings and the belief that Johnson was hiding the real story of the war led to extreme opinions and actions, both by those in favor of the war and by those opposed to it.

Executive War

The United States entered the Vietnam War in 1965 as if it were two separate wars. President Johnson first agreed to fight an air war. With Rolling Thunder, the United States engaged in continuous bombing against North Vietnam. On April 1, 1965, Johnson decided to fight a ground war in South Vietnam to make sure the Saigon government did not collapse. At this stage it was largely the South Vietnamese who were fighting the Viet Cong. The ground war in the south appeared to be between the southern communists, supported by the north, and the southern regime, while the air war pitted the United States against the north.

The American public was confused by all of this, and Johnson's political strategy made it worse. The president wanted to fight an "executive war" in Vietnam. Defense Secretary McNamara claimed that the executive, or president, is allowed to "fight a limited war, to go to war without arousing the public ire." He explained that such a strategy was "almost a necessity in our history, because this is the kind of war we'll likely be facing for the next fifty years."

As historian Barbara Tuchman noted, such a war goes

directly against the principles of American democracy. She wrote that the idea of executive war required "discarding the principle of representative government," because neither the people nor their representatives in Congress were asked to approve or deny a declaration of war.

Decisions about the war rested in the hands of the president and his administration, and Johnson routinely tried to disguise his actions. Even the decision to actually go to war was hidden in the top-secret National Security Action Memorandum 328, of April 6, 1965. Although the purpose of the memo was to approve the use of American ground troops in a combat action, the president still resisted saying that the United States was directly fighting the communists in South Vietnam. This fact was obscured with bureaucratic language: "The President approved the deployment of two additional Marine Battalions and one Marine Air Squadron and associated headquarters and support elements. The President approved a change of mission for all Marine Battalions deployed to Vietnam to permit their more active use under conditions to be established and approved by the Secretary of Defense in consultation with the Secretary of State." The key phrase was "change of mission." It was hardly a stirring call to arms, but this directive hid one of the more controversial, destructive, and important decisions in modern American history.

Public announcement of the top-secret memorandum came two months later, on June 9, and was buried in a White House press release that said the active use of American combat troops would largely be an "increase in effort." The next day Johnson's attorney general, Nicholas D. Katzenbach, assured the president that he did not have to ask for congressional approval to wage this type of war. Katzenbach based his opinion on Johnson's narrow interpretation that he was not declaring war but merely increasing the number of soldiers deployed in Vietnam and enlarging their responsibilities. Johnson hoped that with "one- to two-batallion strength" the soldiers could "attack concentrations of Viet Cong forces."

The president knew that by breaking down his war into innocuous-seeming pieces, he could convince Congress and much of the public that Vietnam was a "limited war." Later, leading American writers and intellectuals would say that the United States had gotten caught in a quagmire by taking a series of small steps that added up to a swamp of total commitment.

In Vietnam, there was never any illusion about a limited commitment. The United States was underwriting the war, and American involvement increased as the south's performance worsened. The Vietnamese expected and received ever greater amounts of aid and weaponry in addition to American combat troops and planes.

One reason Johnson chose to minimalize, if not trivialize, his decision to go to war was that he believed the war would end quickly once the United States became directly involved. But his advisers could not agree on what would constitute an American victory or when the war would end. The disagreements about the methods and aims of the war were so great that when McNamara's deputy John T. McNaughton summarized them, he came up with the following results: "70% — To avoid a humiliating US defeat; 20% — To keep South Viet Nam [and the adjacent] territory from Chinese hands; 10% — To permit the people of

South Viet Nam to enjoy a better, freer way of life; ALSO —
To emerge from crisis without unacceptable taint from
methods used; NOT — to 'help a friend,' although it would be
hard to stay in if asked out."

McNaughton's summary reflects the confusion in the
policy makers' minds. The American commanders in Vietnam wanted to win a military war, and somehow they convinced the president that sending in combat troops would
reduce the risk of a "humiliating US defeat." But in fact the
opposite was true. If American soldiers had not been fighting a war, they obviously could not have been defeated; and
if U.S. troops had stayed out of Vietnam, Hanoi would have
defeated only the army of Saigon.

Not all segments of the government accepted these different aims of the war in Vietnam. The Central Intelligence
Agency already had reported to the president that the domino theory could not be proven, and that in all likelihood it
was wrong. They reported that he need not worry about all
of Southeast Asia, the Pacific, or the West Coast of the
United States falling to the communists if North Vietnam
won the war. Instead the CIA believed that if South Vietnam
and Laos lost to their communist opponents, only the neighboring country of Cambodia would become communist.
That assessment was later proved correct.

In other secret memos officials raised a serious question. Did the United States believe it was fighting to save the
world for democracy, thereby emphasizing the constructive
goal of building democratic institutions around the globe?
Or was it holding the line against further communist expansion, implying that the United States was willing to take up
arms in any country where local communists were poised to

take over a government? Finally, the goal accepted within the Johnson administration was to convince Hanoi to give up its idea of unifying Vietnam under communist control. The United States was not fighting to defeat Hanoi and replace its regime with another. The purpose of the bombings in the north and of the American troops fighting for the south was to preserve a divided Vietnam.

The military strategy devised to fulfill this goal was called a "war of attrition," one that would wear down the enemy until he gave up. The air war was aimed at cutting off the Ho Chi Minh Trail, the north's route for sending men and supplies to the south to aid the Viet Cong. Once those supplies were cut off, the Viet Cong could be defeated by U.S. ground troops. The American military planners presumed there was a limited, finite number of Viet Cong and that by killing off enough of them or preventing them from being replaced by northerners, the United States could prevent the collapse of the Saigon government. To measure the success of this war of attrition, the U.S. military used the "body count" — the number of Viet Cong soldiers killed. The more Viet Cong deaths reported, the greater the American hopes for eliminating the Viet Cong and therefore ending the threat of a united Vietnam under the control of Hanoi.

This strategy led to such anomalies as American soldiers fighting fiercely to capture a Viet Cong outpost and then abandoning it to their South Vietnamese allies, who would then give it up to the Viet Cong again. The American aim was not to hold territory, only to kill Viet Cong. This strategy was not easily understood by American soldiers and pilots, who often found it a deeply suspect way to wage war.

Eventually some became so frustrated by a war that lacked the traditional purposes of defeating the enemy or winning territory that they rebelled against their own army.

Because of international constraints, President Johnson encouraged the ambiguity of the war's aims and strategy. Few of America's allies in Europe actively supported the war, and they all feared that declaring war against Hanoi and fighting to the death would lead to active Chinese or even Soviet involvement, which could trigger a nuclear war.

"Nam" — Americans in Vietnam

A few months before the first marines landed in Da Nang, the respected newspaper columnist Joseph Kraft wrote a dispatch from Saigon describing the scene the soldiers would encounter. "The symbol of the whole [American] operation is the main Saigon PX. It is a metropolitan department store with cigarettes, whiskey, clothing, books, tape recorders, cameras, records, furniture, tennis rackets, broilers, refrigerators, and all the other appurtenances of gracious living in the affluent society."

Kraft found this disturbing. "Thus organized and equipped, the government forces and their American advisors are inevitably set apart from the population. Hardly any of the American advisors even speak the language. . . . As to the Vietnamese army [of the south], far from being a collection of the 'sons of the people,' it has become something like a privileged caste. Its soldiers drive pell-mell through villages, taking food and roughing up the population. . . . And whenever there is fighting, the bombing of villages and the inevitable harm done to innocent civilians only widen the gap between the people and the military."

Kraft was one of the very few American journalists who predicted disaster in Vietnam from the beginning. His voice was drowned out by the great majority who wrote about the hope the newly arriving GIs were bringing to the people of South Vietnam. General William Westmoreland devised the strategy they were to follow to win the war. He declared that they were "not to conquer North Vietnam but to eliminate the insurgency inside South Vietnam." To that end they were to help their ally, ARVN, or the Army of the Republic of Vietnam, to "secure enclaves," then "engage in offensive operations and deep patrolling cooperation with the ARVN," and finally to "provide a reserve when ARVN units needed help and also conduct long-range offensive operations."

The American men sent to fight this war left a rich record of frustration and incomprehension in their memoirs. The GIs wondered out loud if Westmoreland's strategy was built on sand, since ARVN did not want to fight the war; the U.S. troops were the doughnut and ARVN the hole. Certainly the GIs found courageous exceptions, and many patriotic South Vietnamese worked hard to find an alternative to being taken over by communist Vietnamese. But they were not represented by the Saigon government nor by the South Vietnamese army.

Philip Caputo, a marine who fought in the ground war, wrote about his time in Vietnam in *A Rumor of War*. He was one of the first marines to land on the beach in South Vietnam and one of the first to fight under Westmoreland's static defense strategy of protecting American enclaves. Caputo was flabbergasted by what he saw; instead of barbed wire, forts, or any sign of the enemy, his deceptive first impression was that he had landed in paradise: "The 'Communist

Stronghold' in front of us reminded me of a tropical park. Groves of bamboo and coconut palm rose out of rice paddies like islands from a jade-colored sea."

Those first weeks, even the first months, seemed out of another time. When Caputo took occasional "liberty," or time off, he would go to the Grand Hotel Tourane in Da Nang, where he experienced some of the charm of the old French colonial days. He sat on the hotel veranda, drank "cold beer beneath slowly twirling fans and watched sampans gliding down the Tourane River, rust-red in the sunset." It reminded him of the "romantic flavor of [Rudyard] Kipling's colonial wars . . . the 'splendid little war.'" His feelings were matched by the enthusiasm of his fellow soldiers. At the beginning victory seemed possible; he was convinced that "Asian guerrillas did not stand a chance against U.S. Marines."

Caputo's marines were stationed on the coast to provide support for ARVN, which had the main role in defeating the Viet Cong. In July 1965 Secretary of Defense McNamara came to South Vietnam for a four-day visit to assess these first months of direct American involvement. He agreed to support Westmoreland's secret request to increase the number of American troops to 275,000 from the thirty-four battalions, or some 100,000 soldiers, that the president had originally approved. Just one month earlier, Westmoreland had said he needed 175,000 men; now the number was higher by 100,000.

McNamara asked Johnson to grant this dramatic increase even though it meant that some five hundred American men could be killed each month. But, he wrote, "United States public opinion will support this course of action because it is a sensible and courageous military-political program designed and likely to bring about a success in Vietnam." This was the last time McNamara was optimistic about American policy in Vietnam.

The marines and the army, joined by the other branches of the American armed services, the navy and the air force, set up headquarters in South Vietnam in 1965. The navy patrolled the coastal waters, and by year's end had moved into the rivers as well. The air force bombed not only the north but also suspected communist strongholds in the south.

It was a heady time for the American troops. Westmoreland convinced Johnson not only to raise the number of Americans fighting in Vietnam, but also to let them have a freer hand. This allowed them to expand Westmoreland's search-and-destroy strategy by going on the offensive. The soldiers were ordered to go out and find the enemy, either Viet Cong or the North Vietnamese army (NVA), and engage them in combat.

Philip Caputo took part in the first engagements with the communists. He fought at what the Americans called Happy Valley, at the foot of the Central Highlands, a mountainous area and known hideout of the Viet Cong and NVA in the South. When Caputo, an officer, was in charge of a company on a routine patrol in search of the enemy, they nearly stumbled into battle and had to call in reinforcements. Caputo's company was in the rear, watching B Company in action. "It was as though we were in an open-air theater, watching a war movie," he wrote. "The marines running at a crouch into the helicopters; the helicopters taking off one by one as they were loaded, each rising in a floating, nose-down climb out of the dust cloud raised by the rotor blades."

That engagement led to a briefing for all officers to discuss the rules of engagement in this new type of war. The question raised was how one distinguishes the Vietnamese "enemy" from the Vietnamese civilian. The officer in charge said that "no fire [should] be directed at unarmed Vietnamese unless they were running. A running Vietnamese was a fair target."

Caputo was bewildered. "No one was eager to shoot civilians," he wrote. He also wanted to know if someday a GI could be court-martialed for shooting a running Vietnamese. His superior answered, "Look, I don't know what this is supposed to mean, but . . . they said that as far as they're concerned, if he's dead and Vietnamese, he's VC [Viet Cong]."

As Caputo and his marines were going out on search-and-destroy operations, Robert Mason, who later wrote a memoir called *Chickenhawk*, arrived in Vietnam to pilot the helicopters that would transform modern warfare. Helicopters replaced trucks and ambulances, transporting troops quickly to battle fronts that were inaccessible by road and carrying out the wounded from those areas. They also were flown over the countryside to discover where the enemy was hiding. In attacks, helicopters complemented the firepower of troops on the ground and of bombers far overhead. Helicopters became the workhorses of the war, and pilots like Mason got used to twenty-hour days flying above treetops, in and out of fire fights, and into landing zones under attack by the enemy.

The first year of the war, helicopters were the miracle workers as well. When Mason arrived in September 1965, the war already had lost the innocence Caputo had found six months earlier. Mason saw Vietnam first in the rainy season, when "small-arms fire popped and crackled in the darkness." The war was no longer hidden behind the veil of paradise.

Mason's first contact with the Vietnamese was also more ominous than Caputo's. Put in charge of a work crew helping construct a camp, he was warned that "obviously some of the people in the work crew are VC." Even though he found it puzzling that the Viet Cong could so easily infiltrate this American redoubt, he kept his eyes open, and at the end of the project discovered "discreet signs for VCs to sabotage the encampment."

By October Mason was also flying into Happy Valley in Operation Silver Bayonet, the first major American campaign against the enemy. Mason flew troop lifts, helping to ferry in the 2,500 GIs fighting there. From his vantage point the fight was nearly even. "The VC always knew which clearing we would use for a landing zone," he complained. Moreover, the military intelligence people never seemed to get the right information. Soldiers sent out to fight the Viet Cong often "turned up nothing."

Nonetheless, the first weeks of that battle were a success for the Americans, and when Mason went down to Saigon for R & R (rest and relaxation) he found an American newsmagazine that praised the U.S. soldiers for preventing a defeat for the South Vietnamese army. However, this made Mason uneasy. "The article did not say a word about our effectiveness," he wrote. "With all our mobility, the VC still called the shots. We fought on their terms."

That November, at the Battle of Ia Drang, Mason found out whether the Americans could win when fighting on the communists' terms. There, in the western part of the Central Highlands along the Cambodian-Vietnamese border, the Americans had their first contest against the regular army of North Vietnam.

Mason remembered one of the first mornings of that campaign. "That day was bright. Deep blue skies blazed over the shrub-covered hills and valleys of elephant grass." He was alert. His superior told him, "Keep your eyes open. The net is beginning to tighten up . . . [the enemy] might get fidgety."

Everyone was nervous; it was real war. Mason was in and out of the battle. He landed once and "turned around and saw a confused-looking private walking through the swirling smoke with the head of someone he knew held by the hair." Mason wondered if he had to carry the head on the helicopter. (He did.) Soldiers were crying as their buddies died. That night Mason landed in a zone that appeared quiet. "The NVA had allowed us to land without opposition. . . . When they were sure we were on the ground and busy, they opened up."

In the middle of the campaign, Mason and the others realized they were winning. Not only were they killing the enemy, they had figured out where they could find three North Vietnamese regiments. Mason wrote that at the end of one day of heavy fighting, "the thunder [of the cannons] stopped, the quiet was startling. . . . A hit. Body count over 150."

When the battle of Ia Drang Valley was over, the count was even more impressive: 1,200 enemy dead, compared to 200 U.S. soldiers. The Americans had won. This victory should have been a moment of glory and confidence for the Americans, but instead Westmoreland said it revealed the disquieting fact that the North Vietnamese communists were sending troops south at a far greater rate than he had anticipated. Westmoreland asked the president for authorization to send an additional 168,000 U.S. troops to Vietnam, raising the overall force to 443,000.

According to American intelligence reports, the number of communist troops in the south had risen from 48,550 in July 1965 to some 63,550 troops by November. By the end of the year there were eight North Vietnamese regiments, or 4,800 soldiers, in the south. The news cast doubts on the effectiveness of the American strategy. The air war was not preventing infiltration from the north, nor was the ground war reducing the number of southerners fighting with the Viet Cong.

American officials had not expected the Vietnamese communists to be so successful. In November 1965 the Defense Intelligence Agency prepared a secret report on the effectiveness of the American bombing of North Vietnam. It said that while the bombing was "reducing the industrial performance" of the north, this was of little consequence, since the north had few industries. "The idea that destroying, or threatening to destroy, North Vietnam's industry would pressure Hanoi into calling it quits seems, in retrospect, a colossal misjudgment," the report said.

According to the report, North Vietnam received most of the military equipment it needed from the Soviet Union and China. That equipment was sent south on roads and trails that were "inherently flexible." That is, if one section of the complex network of paths and roads called the Ho Chi Minh Trail was bombed, porters and soldiers would be diverted to another section and continue down to the south.

The report warned that the bombing would not stop the north from sending even more equipment and troops. The Vietnamese communists were so poor and their economy so primitive that they had to fight without great expense. For example, they used local supplies as much as possible, and when those supplies ran out they simply did not fight. The report concluded that "supporting the war in the South was hardly a great strain on North Vietnam's economy."

Officials in Vietnam and in Washington knew the American war strategy had to change.

Escalate and Demonstrate

President Johnson was of two minds on what to do in Vietnam. At Christmas he temporarily halted the bombing of North Vietnam, saying that he wanted to negotiate an end to the war. He sent his representatives around the world to spread this message and seek foreign reactions. During this thirty-seven-day bombing halt, Johnson also made plans to escalate American involvement in Vietnam if his offers to negotiate were rejected.

At this juncture neither the United States nor North Vietnam wanted to compromise. As one American intelligence assessment reported, the American bombing had increased rather than diminished the Vietnamese communists' will to fight. The Hanoi government had doubled its imports of military equipment and had begun building "one of the strongest air defense concentrations in the world," according to historian Stanley Karnow. They had decided to match the American intervention with their own form of escalation.

Although the communists were considered a guerrilla force, the North Vietnamese realized in late 1965 that they had to respond to the American entry into the war with technologically advanced conventional war strategies. The Viet Cong in the south largely relied on guerrilla tactics — booby traps and hit-and-run engagements — but the North Vietnamese traveled and fought like a regular army. They respected the superiority of the American army in conventional warfare and avoided battles with U.S. units, targeting instead ARVN, Saigon's army, the weak arm of the American fighting force. The North Vietnamese wisely maneuvered around the new Goliaths and continued pounding their real target — the South Vietnamese regime.

In January 1966 one of McNamara's most trusted aides, Assistant Secretary of Defense John T. McNaughton, wrote another assessment of the war to help his boss figure out alternative strategies. The report, entitled "Some Paragraphs on Vietnam," was devastating. Quite baldly McNaughton stated that "we . . . have in Vietnam the ingredients of an enormous miscalculation." He listed all the obvious defects in the policy that others, particularly Westmoreland, had tried to deny.

- The Saigon army, ARVN, was "tired, passive and accommodation-prone," meaning that they didn't fight.

- The communists were "effectively matching our deployments"; no matter how many Viet Cong were killed in action, there were always more to replace them.

- The bombing of the north might or might not stop the flow of men and arms to the south.

- Pacification, or winning the political loyalties of the South Vietnamese people, was not working "despite efforts and hopes."

- The South Vietnam government's "political infrastructure [was] moribund and weaker than the VC infrastructure among most of the rural population." The Viet Cong were running the countryside.

- "South Vietnam [was] near the edge of serious inflation and economic chaos."

Although McNaughton had put together a nearly hopeless litany of failure, he did not believe that the United States should give up. He underlined America's "objective" in Vietnam, which he said was "to avoid humiliation." He dismissed the idea that the United States was fighting to save a friend, deny the communists a victory, or prevent other countries from falling to communism. "The reasons why we went into Vietnam to the present depth are varied," he wrote, "but they are now largely academic. Why we have not withdrawn from Vietnam is, by all odds, one reason: . . . To preserve our reputation as a guarantor, and thus to preserve our effectiveness in the rest of the world. . . . The ante is now very high. It is important that we behave so as to protect our reputation."

McNaughton's "best judgment" was that even with vastly increased American troop strength, the situation would never allow anything more than a stalemate. "We will probably be faced in early 1967 with a continued stalemate at a higher level of forces and casualties," he wrote. Then he proposed that the United States begin planning for something "short of victory": a neutral South Vietnam, an anti-

American government in the south, or even a South Vietnam that had "succumbed to the VC or the North."

The conclusion was a blunt warning wrapped in bureaucratic language. "We are in a dilemma. . . . The risk is that it may be that the coin must come up heads or tails, not on the edge." One side would win and the other would lose; the memo leaves no doubt who McNaughton thought would be the winner.

From later events it is clear McNaughton's memo had a deep impact on his boss, Secretary of Defense McNamara, but not on Johnson. The president went full steam ahead. In February he held a conference in Honolulu with his senior advisers and the new leaders of South Vietnam, President Nguyen Van Thieu and Prime Minister Nguyen Cao Ky.

These two officers had climbed to the top by pushing aside all civilian leaders and running the country like a junta. About the time the American marines were landing in Da Nang the previous spring, the old government had fallen and the bright-eyed Ky had become South Vietnam's leader. Thieu, the president, played only a ceremonial role at first. When McNamara visited the country in November 1965, he reported that the "Ky government of generals is surviving, but not acquiring wide support or generating action."

Ky and Thieu were new faces, not yet associated with defeat or humiliation for the United States. That November the Americans had put a finger in the dike of the communist offensive with their victory at Ia Drang, and the South Vietnamese government had also basked in the victory. When Johnson met Ky and Thieu in Honolulu he wanted to believe in them; the South Vietnamese leaders had come to Honolulu prepared to meet Johnson's expectations. According to historian Stanley Karnow, Ky's speech, written by his American adviser, was aimed at impressing Johnson with its populist message, promising to carry out a "social revolution" in South Vietnam that would bring "respect and dignity" to every citizen.

A communique was signed whereby the South Vietnamese agreed to institute American-style reforms in their war-torn land. Johnson called the document "a kind of bible that we are going to follow. When we come back here ninety days from now, or six months from now, we are going to start out and [ask] . . . how have you built democracy in the rural area? How much of it have you built, when and where? Give us dates, times, numbers." Johnson had Ky and Thieu promise to make the government more efficient, to improve health care, and to bring electric power to rural areas. And in the president's unmistakable way, he said, "Are those just phrases, high-sounding words, or do you have coonskins on the wall?"

Immediately afterward, events suggested that the South Vietnamese generals understood political maneuvering better than electrifying impoverished villages. Ky interpreted Johnson's words of praise and encouragement as a personal endorsement, and upon his return to Saigon he got rid of one of his strongest rivals, a popular Buddhist general named Nguyen Chanh Thi. However, Thi refused to accept his ouster, and soon Buddhists were demonstrating in Da Nang to keep the general in the government. When South Vietnamese paratroopers in the Da Nang area joined the Buddhists in protest, Ky sent his own South Vietnamese marines to "liberate" the city. But the protesters resisted, and Ky was forced to promise in writing to keep Thi in the government and not punish demonstrators.

But as soon as he got his troops in order, Ky went back on his word and sent in a far larger attack force against Da Nang's Buddhists. McNamara called this "pacification," but in fact Ky was quelling a rebellion by mutinous troops who saw no reason why he should kick out a good general. Ky was supposed to be "pacifying" the Viet Cong–held countryside.

The protestors multiplied into a mass "struggle movement" demanding elections and democracy, which Ky had promised Johnson he would arrange. But Ky refused to meet the protestors' demands, thereby breaking his word to the American president. This was the last significant challenge to the government in the south. The middle ground between the Saigon military and the Viet Cong had been destroyed.

The options McNaughton had listed for South Vietnam were narrowing. With Ky's maneuvers there was no longer hope for neutrality and no reason to imagine an anti-American government in the south.

These internecine South Vietnamese battles were not welcome news to the president or to the increasingly bewildered American public. New voices were being heard in the streets, the voices of young people and a few respected national figures protesting against America's involvement in the Vietnam War. Antiwar demonstrations were becoming a new political institution. On April 17, 1965, the Students for a Democratic Society (SDS) held an antiwar march in Washington, D.C., that drew some 20,000 to 25,000 people, setting a record for the largest peace march in American history.

The size of the crowd was even more remarkable because few famous people led the march, which took place near the White House. Among those speaking was the SDS president, Paul Potter, who said, "We must accept the consequences that calling for an end of the war in Vietnam is in fact allowing for the likelihood that a Vietnam without war will be a self-styled communist Vietnam. I must say to you that I would rather see Vietnam communist than see it under continuous subjugation or the ruin that American domination has brought."

At this beginning stage of the protest movement, the leaders were bold in their appraisals and frank about the consequences of withdrawing from Vietnam. They said they preferred to let the communists have Vietnam than to drop any more bombs on the country. Potter's public analysis, which was very close to the government's secret predictions, led him to conclude that the American involvement would bring only death and destruction to South Vietnam, not a victory for democracy. It was the bombardment of the countryside, the "ruin" that Potter mentioned, that most disturbed these activists and many other, more moderate Americans.

Photographs from the battlefield accompanied stories of destruction on a large scale. When U.S. Representative Clement Zablocki, a supporter of the war, traveled to South Vietnam in February 1966, he wrote a report for the House Foreign Affairs Committee saying that two Vietnamese civilians were being killed for every Viet Cong and in some cases as many as six civilians for every enemy soldier.

This was not the image of the war that the politicians wanted American citizens to have. Ambassador Lodge, reappointed to head the embassy in Saigon after the 1964 presidential election, was asked to respond to the Zablocki report. He basically confirmed the findings but said that this casualty rate was necessary because of America's policy of using its superior firepower, which "lies largely in almost unlimited quantities of sophisticated equipment of war. We have weapons of tremendous power, ranging from B-52's [bombers], 175 [millimeter] guns, and 8-inch naval guns, down to rapid firing M-16 rifles. . . . Although extreme caution is used when they are employed it is inevitable that they will produce civilian casualties, most of which we will never learn about."

Lodge argued that if this firepower were restricted in order to reduce civilian casualties, the United States would lose its superiority. He used this example: "How do you learn whether anyone was inside structures and sampans destroyed by the hundreds every day by air strikes, artillery fire and naval gunfire? Even if you find casualties in them, how do you know whether they were innocent civilians or VC?"

This sort of argument fed the antiwar movement's claim that the ends did not justify the means in the Vietnam conflict. In the early years of protest, 1965 and 1966, the antiwar movement attracted support from a diverse range of Americans, but especially from those people who felt most threatened by the draft. A sociologist's poll taken at that time showed that the "hawks," those who supported the war, were "concentrated among the college-educated high-income strata." The "doves," those against the war, tended to be less well educated and less wealthy, lower-paid professionals, white-collar and blue-collar workers. The American army fighting the war was recruited or drafted from such lower-class families.

This period of passionate protest was both nonviolent

and nonideological. One act was particularly symbolic of those times. On November 2, 1965, a thirty-two-year-old Quaker pacifist named Norman Morrison left his Maryland home and drove to Washington, D.C. He went to the Pentagon and stood near the window of Secretary of Defense McNamara, who had been singled out by the protestors as the war's chief architect. Morrison poured gasoline over his body and set himself on fire. His suicide by immolation was the same protest made by some pacifist Buddhists in South Vietnam.

His death was memorialized in the poem "Norman Morrison" by David Ferguson, who wrote that Morrison "spoke in a tongue of flame near the Pentagon where they had no doubt. Other people's pain can turn so easily into a kind of play."

Poets and other intellectuals questioned whether the Johnson administration could demand support for the war from American citizens on the basis of patriotism. Since the 1950s, when Europe and Asia had divided along communist and noncommunist lines, the American public had largely applauded their nation's support of democracy against communism, indeed were proud of it. The Vietnam War began to stand out as the awful exception, as the one American policy that some citizens opposed strongly enough to risk their jobs or even, in some cases, their citizenship; a few, like Morrison, gave their lives to protest.

As the streets filled with protestors in 1965 and 1966, some of America's leaders felt uneasy about their positions on the war. In April 1967 Dr. Martin Luther King, Jr., the recipient of the Nobel Prize for Peace for his nonviolent protests against American racism and segregation, took a public stand against the war. King had been thinking about the Vietnam issue for two troubled years but had pushed aside his doubts and heeded his supporters, who told him to concentrate on affairs at home. But the war was having such an impact on the lives of black Americans that King felt he could no longer be silent. At Riverside Church in New York City, King described how the military buildup in Vietnam was taking money, talent, and energy away from the programs needed to help the poor.

"We were taking the young black men who had been crippled by our society and sending them eight thousand miles away to guarantee liberties in Southeast Asia which they had not found in Southwest Georgia and East Harlem," he said. "So we have been repeatedly faced with the cruel irony of watching Negro and white boys on TV screens as they kill and die together for a nation that has been unable to seat them together in the same schools."

King, a man dedicated to nonviolence, talked about the hypocrisy he saw. "We are adding cynicism to the process of death, for our troops must know after a short period there that none of the things we claim to be fighting for are really involved. I speak as a child of God and brother to the suffering poor of Vietnam and the poor of America who are paying the double price of smashed hopes at home and death and corruption in Vietnam."

King also talked about the devastating effect the war was having on the people of Southeast Asia. "[The South Vietnamese] people read our leaflets and received regular promises of peace and democracy — and land reform. Now they languish under our bombs and consider us — not their fellow Vietnamese — the real enemy. They move sadly and apathetically as we herd them off the land of their fathers into concentration camps where minimal social needs are rarely met. They know they must move or be destroyed by our bombs. So they go. They watch as we poison their water, as we kill a million acres of their crops. They must weep as the bulldozers destroy their precious trees." This, he said, was not the way to fight communism. "We must not engage in a negative anticommunism, but rather in a positive thrust for democracy."

King advocated halting the American bombing and instituting a cease-fire. He thought that the NLF should have a role in the postwar government of South Vietnam, and that a date should be set for all foreign troops to leave, in accordance with the 1954 Geneva Accords. He ended his speech with this anguished warning: "If we do not act we shall surely be dragged down the long, dark and shameful corridors of time reserved for those who possess power without compassion, might without morality, and strength without sight. . . . The choice is ours, and though we might prefer it otherwise we *must* choose in this crucial moment of human history." King remained one of the most persuasive voices in the antiwar movement until his assassination in 1968.

Another leader who spoke against the war was the renowned pediatrician Dr. Benjamin Spock. Like King, he broke with friends and colleagues who told him that his position was unpatriotic. Spock said that as a physician for young people he thought it "no longer sufficient to protect children from just the familiar physical diseases. . . . Now the greatest danger to life — by far — is from nuclear disaster." Fear that the Vietnam War would trigger a nuclear war was growing as the level of destruction rose.

The protest movement against the Vietnam War had no precedent in American history in its size and breadth and the extremes to which some protestors went. The movement grew into an examination of the entire society, characterized as much by actions as words. There were marches down the streets of the nation's cities, sit-ins on college campuses, teach-ins to debate the war, demonstrations against government policy in front of official buildings. Students of the era learned how to apply for permission to hold marches on city streets and memorized the limits of lawful demonstration.

Many protestors were willing to break laws, too. One of the first issues that led to unlawful action was the draft. American men were eligible to be drafted into the U.S. army at the age of eighteen. When they received their draft notice, if they were not rejected for physical or other reasons, the men had several options. They could accept the draft and become a private in the army, with a good chance of being sent to fight in Vietnam; they could volunteer for another branch of the armed services, with a better chance to avoid going to Vietnam; they could win a deferment of military service by continuing a college education, for example; or they could refuse to serve and either go to jail or go into hiding.

As soon as American soldiers were sent to war in Vietnam and began dying in the paddy fields, young men in the United States started searching for ways to avoid military service. In all, more than half of those eligible for service — or 15 million men out of 27 million — asked for and won draft deferments. Those from "disadvantaged backgrounds were about twice as likely as their better-off peers to serve in the military, go to Vietnam and see combat," according to a

1977 University of Notre Dame study. The sons of officials waging the war rarely were sent to the battlefield. And the accusation of injustice in the draft was added to the lengthening list of reasons why protestors felt the United States should get out of Vietnam.

Early on, young men who were opposed to America's war in Vietnam were exhorted to throw away their draft cards or refuse to register at all for military service, to take part in "draft resistance." Beginning in 1966 young men stood up at public demonstrations and tore up or burned their draft cards. Some 5,000 draft cards were destroyed at protests. A resistance manifesto of sorts was written in October 1967 by a group of young men about to give back their draft cards. "We will hand in our draft cards and refuse any further cooperation with the Selective Service System. By doing so we will actively challenge the government's right to draft American men for its criminal war against the people of Vietnam. We of the Resistance feel that we can no longer passively acquiesce to the Selective Service System by accepting its deferments."

Eventually over half a million men refused to serve; some went into hiding in the United States, others fled the country. More than half of those who fled went north to Canada. It was the largest mass exodus from the United States since America's Revolutionary War, when the defeated Tories also escaped to Canada. Another 250,000 young men never registered for the draft and were never caught. Another 172,000 became conscientious objectors.

Not all of the 15 million men who won draft deferments were committed antiwar protestors. Unlike World War II when nearly all young Americans wanted to fight and become heroes, some just were not convinced the war was worth risking their life, and some families refused to send their sons off to battle and instead sent them to college. Underneath the protest movement was a silent majority who did not actively support the war. The privilege of deferment, which was unavailable to many men from poor and disadvantaged backgrounds, pitted young men against each other. One major newspaper called the Vietnam War a "generation-wide catastrophe."

The soldiers fighting the war, whether they believed in it or not, were bitter about the deferments and the increasingly loud protests at home. Private John P. Murphy wrote this letter home to a friend. "Dear Fran, You asked me if I am bitter. I'm afraid so. Why shouldn't I be? I mean, here I am trying to kill all the Communists, and there you are with the immature nuts trying to help them out [protesting the war]. . . . I get sick to my guts every time I see a man lying there without his limbs. . . . I've got the hurt. The hurt of all the burnt-out villages and the naked kids and the lepers and the stink of the dead." The protests were sapping morale at home and in the battlefield.

Music became part of the way young Americans addressed the issue of war and protest. Todd Gitlin, historian of and participant in the antiwar movement, believes that the August 1965 release of the record "Eve of Destruction" by Barry McGuire marked a symbolic shift in the movement. When McGuire sang that young people were old enough to kill but not allowed to vote, that they said they didn't believe in war but then carried guns in Vietnam, young people listened. Almost all of the music of the era meshed with the new drug scene, which began with the new popularity of marijuana, or pot. Simple protest soon turned to resistance, and added to that was "drugs, sex and rock 'n' roll." Gitlin called this the "express train of antiauthority [which] was hard to break."

The resistance movement among young people seemed to accelerate the breaking of old mores just as the war exploded with a sharp increase in the casualty rate and in the tonnage of bombs dropped. A parallel seemed to develop between the war and the splintering of American society. From 1965 until 1967 some 15,000 Americans died in Vietnam. During those same years, 277,757 South Vietnamese died, and 390,865 were wounded; over 4 million Vietnamese became refugees. (The North Vietnamese and Viet Cong casualty figures are incomplete.) In 1966 and 1967 the United States spent $25.9 billion on the war; the air war alone cost $6.57 billion. During this period the United States dropped 1,292,413 tons of bombs.

This was also the time of milestone marches against the war. The October 1965 marches, attended by 15,000 to 20,000 neatly attired protestors, were topped by a 1967 march in New York that drew nearly 500,000 people, many dressed irreverently. Marching, protesting, and demonstrating against the Vietnam War had become part of a new youth culture.

In South Vietnam, Westmoreland's strategy of escalating American involvement to help ARVN reclaim control of the countryside was failing. His methods of warfare were being criticized as much as the destruction that was being wrought. Once the U.S. army realized that ARVN could not hold the territory won by American soldiers, the commanders followed a new tactic of "denying" territory to the enemy, which in practice often meant destroying it.

Almost 9 percent of the bombs dropped on South Vietnam carried napalm, a jellylike substance that burned whatever it touched — forests, villages, farmland, or people. Napalm was dropped over areas in the south that the military called "free bombing zones" to be denied to the enemy. Several historians believe that American public opinion was turned against the war as much by seeing photographs and television coverage of napalm-scarred children as by the antiwar marches.

In his book *The Village of Ben Suc,* Jonathan Schell described how a once prosperous village of 3,500 South Vietnamese, with a history going back to the late eighteenth century, was systematically destroyed in January 1967 by the U.S. army to prevent its capture by the Viet Cong. The soldiers gave the villagers a few hours to gather their belongings — pots and pans, clothing, animals, tools — and prepare to leave their homes forever. The village men suspected of being Viet Cong were taken away as prisoners. The remaining villagers slept one last night in their homes and were trucked off to a refugee camp the following morning.

Schell described the last moments of Ben Suc. "The villagers crouched along the road with their bundles of belongings while American infantrymen ducked in and out of the palm groves behind them, some pouring gasoline on the grass roofs of the houses and others going from house to house setting them afire." The village was burned down; the rice paddies and orchards of mangoes, jackfruit, and grapefruit were destroyed. Within one week the entire area was torched and bulldozed and the trees uprooted. Then American jets flew over and bombed the ground, scorching the ruins of houses and rubble until nothing was left.

The village of Ben Suc was in the path of Operation Cedar Falls, in the Saigon River area, where the U.S. military also destroyed other villages, like Rach Kien Bung Cong and Rach Bap, to deny them to the enemy. The people who had lived in those towns became refugees. When they reached the poorly prepared camps that were to be their makeshift homes, they became extremely disillusioned, which often convinced them to help the Viet Cong.

More than one historian has noted this irony. George C. Herring wrote that while President Johnson wanted to be remembered in Vietnam for helping the farmers, for building schools and developing agriculture, his war had the opposite effect: people were forced into the cities, where they lived either in "dirty refugee camps" or the "seedy sprawl" of shanty towns surrounding the cities, especially Saigon.

Many South Vietnamese said they had no choice but to flee to Saigon to escape the bombing. One group of refugees explained that American planes dropped leaflets warning that "the wicked Viet Cong have stored weapons and supplies in your village. Soon naval gunfire is going to be conducted on your village to destroy these Viet Cong supplies. We ask that you take cover as we do not wish to kill innocent people."

These villagers left rather than taking cover and risking injury. One of them said, "You tell us that the purpose of the bombs is to destroy the supplies of the Viet Cong — yet they can move their supplies much faster than we can move buffalo, pigs, chickens, rice, furniture, and children. If we take the time to gather our belongings we will be killed. Most of us just hurry away without those things precious to us."

Even Johnson's attempt at direct economic aid to farmers ran aground because most of the money, which was administered by the Saigon government, was used to enrich city dwellers and never sent on to the villages. The gap between the rich and poor in Vietnam grew on the billions the United States paid to keep the war going. Refugees and villagers flocked to the capital as the only source of wealth and safety. By 1967 Saigon was said to have the highest population density of any city in the world — twice that of Tokyo.

The Consensus Crumbles

Two years after troops began active combat duty in Vietnam, American society was angrily divided over the war. The draft calls in the summer of 1967 exceeded 30,000 each month, reaching into families previously untouched by the war. In August Johnson announced a 10 percent surtax on the federal income tax to pay for the war. This became a regular reminder to rich and poor that the war was hurting their pocketbooks. A poll taken in October showed that only 28 percent of Americans approved of the way Johnson was carrying out the war.

In the battlefield the consensus was crumbling as well. Among the first groups to openly express disenchantment were black Americans, who found themselves disproportionately assigned to dangerous frontline combat duty. At the end of the Second World War, blacks accounted for 12 percent of combat soldiers. When the Vietnam War began, they made up 31 percent of the combat forces. In the first year of fighting, 24 percent of those killed were black.

Blacks and other minorities were more likely to be drafted than whites. Military records show that more than 30 percent of qualified blacks were drafted, as opposed to less than 19 percent of qualified whites. Laurence M. Baskir and William A. Strauss said in *Chance and Circumstance* that while it is difficult to compare social, economic, and racial discrimination in Vietnam to that in other wars, "the American people were never before as conscious of how unevenly the obligation to serve was distributed." They quoted an American general in Vietnam, who said, "In the average rifle company, the strength was 50% composed of Negroes, Southwestern Mexicans, Puerto Ricans, Guamanians, Nisei [Japanese Americans], and so on. But a real cross-section of American youth? Almost never."

To its credit, the Defense Department recognized this as a major problem and acted to reduce the number of minorities in combat duty, but the problem went deeper. In Vietnam, racial discrimination raised tensions in combat units, which were integrated for the first time in U.S. military history. Author Wallace Terry collected the stories of blacks who served in Vietnam in the book *Bloods*. One man, Specialist 5 Harold "Light Bulb" Bryant, told Terry: "I remember this white guy from Oklahoma. He said that the reason he had volunteered to come over to Vietnam was because he wanted to kill some gooks. He was a typical example of a John Wayne complex." Another white man in Bryant's unit made sure everyone knew he was a member of the Ku Klux Klan. Others flew the Confederate flag. By 1967 black soldiers were upset by the fact that white soldiers who believed that the white race was superior to the black routinely committed barbaric acts. For example, Bryant remembered soldiers who cut off the ears of Viet Cong corpses and strung them on their dogtag chains, and one soldier who violated a female corpse.

Another black soldier, Specialist 4 Richard J. Ford III, was decorated with two Bronze Stars for his duty in combat. "The officers, the generals, and whoever came out to the hospital to see you," he said. "They respected you and pat you on the back. . . . In the States the same officers that pat me on the back wouldn't even speak to me."

Low morale became a problem for whites and blacks as the war continued without any sign of victory. And as morale grew worse, drugs became a problem for soldiers of all races. Ford said his comrades were smoking marijuana and getting high for combat. "In the field most of the guys stayed high. Lot of them couldn't face it." Soon the American armed forces were reporting unusually high rates of absences without leave (AWOL), desertion, and, eventually, small mutinies.

The United States and North Vietnam were no closer to finding a political settlement to the war. Hanoi had reduced its demands to one, an unconditional halt in the bombing before any peace talks. The United States asked that the North Vietnamese promise not to take advantage of such a halt and to stop infiltrating the south. Neither side trusted the other.

By the beginning of 1967 Defense Secretary McNamara began to understand that the war was costing far too much and that his strategies had brought the United States no closer to victory. He admitted that the pacification plan for rural South Vietnam had backfired; the farmers were losing both their land and their faith in the Saigon government. Around this time an argument broke out over the methods that would win the war. General Westmoreland requested 100,000 additional soldiers, and the Joint Chiefs of Staff asked for fifty-seven new bombing targets in North Vietnam.

In response to those requests, McNamara wrote a long memo on May 19, 1967. He argued against the new bombing targets and questioned the entire program. He said bombing had failed to prevent the North Vietnamese from sending men and supplies to South Vietnam. "Our efforts physically to cut the flow meaningfully by actions in North Vietnam therefore largely fail." Moreover, he said that the United States felt the high cost of the bombing as much as, if not more than, North Vietnam; the United States lost one pilot for every forty bombing runs. Then he wrote: "There may be a limit beyond which many Americans and much of the world will not permit the United States to go. The picture of the world's greatest superpower killing or seriously injuring 1,000 noncombatants a week, while trying to pound a tiny backward nation into submission on an issue whose merits are hotly disputed, is not a pretty one."

McNamara also succeeded in limiting Westmoreland's new troops to 50,000, even though he personally believed those 50,000 soldiers would make no difference and the resulting casualties would be for naught. He kept the total number of U.S. soldiers in Vietnam at 525,000.

In a sense, a new McNamara was arguing against the old McNamara. He reminded Johnson what he thought the

American goals were at the beginning of the war. "To the extent that our original intervention and our existing actions in Vietnam were motivated by the perceived need to draw the line against Chinese expansionism in Asia, our objective has already been attained." He reiterated that this was a limited executive war and that the president did not have to accept the advice of the Joint Chiefs, who were making it open-ended.

The shift in public opinion certainly swayed McNamara. He was aware of the antiwar marchers boldly marching through Washington's streets shouting: "Hey, hey, LBJ, how many kids did you kill today?"; of the newspaper editorials questioning the war and the Democratic politicians asking why this was wasn't "working." Representative Thomas P. "Tip" O'Neill exemplified the dissenters in Johnson's own Democratic party, whose objections were not necessarily based on moral or legal grounds but on the fact that the policy had failed. "We are dropping $20,000 bombs every time somebody thinks he sees four Viet Cong in a bush. And it isn't working," O'Neill said. (Intelligence reports backed up O'Neill's complaints. In confidential reports the CIA said that 80 percent of the people killed by the bombing of the north were civilians.)

To limit that bombing, McNamara told the public that the air war was failing. On August 25, 1967, he told a Congressional subcommittee examining the air war that the United States had spent $911 million to destroy $320 million worth of North Vietnamese property without significantly affecting the enemy's ability or will to fight. He said the tons of bombs dropped on the Ho Chi Minh Trail had hit only 2 percent of the soldiers going south. And even though

U.S. bombers had knocked out 85 percent of North Vietnam's electricity plants, the regime quickly replaced them with small diesel generators. Whenever he could, McNamara underlined the fact that North Vietnam was a backward rural nation, not like America's Second World War enemies Germany or Japan, which had industrial bases that could be bombed, thereby altering the course of war. Rather than hitting industrial targets, McNamara pointed out, the bombing had killed 29,000 civilians in the north.

McNamara's testimony was devastating. Afterward Senator Stuart Symington of Missouri said, "If the position as presented by the secretary this morning is right, I believe the United States should get out of Vietnam at the earliest possible time, and on the best possible basis; because with his premises, there would appear to be no chance for any true 'success' in this long war."

That was McNamara's message to Congress and to the president. On November 1, 1967, he made his final, private appeal to Johnson, asking that the bombing of North Vietnam be ended, that no more troops be sent to South Vietnam, and that the war be turned over as much as possible to the South Vietnamese. He also said he wanted to see the number of American casualties and the destruction of Vietnam reduced.

By the end of November Johnson announced that McNamara was leaving the Department of Defense to become president of the World Bank. His departure date was set for March 1, 1968.

As if to underscore his disagreement with McNamara's new doubts about the war, Johnson began what he called a "success offensive" to convince America that the Vietnam

War could be won and that American troops were making great strides toward that goal. Westmoreland flew to Washington and told news reporters, "I am very, very encouraged. I have never been more encouraged in the four years that I have been in Vietnam. We are making real progress. Everyone is encouraged." In a major public speech on November 21 he said, "With 1968, a new phase is now starting. . . . We have reached an important point when the end begins to come into view." General Bruce Palmer, the deputy commander of the U.S. Army in Vietnam, said in an interview: "The Viet Cong has been defeated from Da Nang all the way down in the populated areas. He can't get food and he can't recruit."

Through all of this, McNamara was silent. He embodied what became so frustrating and heartbreaking in the debate over the Vietnam War. Many years later McNamara admitted in sworn testimony that he realized as early as late 1965 that the United States could not win the war, but he did not act on his judgment. When he publicly began advising the nation and Johnson to scale back the commitment in Vietnam and reconsider U.S. goals, McNamara refused to openly challenge the president on war policy. He tried to speak the truth without taking sides, as if he had not been the chief architect of the war he was now questioning. But the man famous for his ability as a "number cruncher" had interpreted the reports correctly. The United States could not win the war in Vietnam. Soon this would be proven in a battle that began during the Vietnamese New Year festival known as Tet.

6

TET AND THE BEGINNING
OF THE END

IMAGINE WHAT THE Vietnamese communists must have thought when the world's greatest superpower risked social peace at home and its good name abroad to defeat them. The countries of Western Europe were counseling the United States to abandon its quest in Vietnam; antiwar activists were traveling to Hanoi to find out why Vietnam was so important to the United States. The Vietnamese communists began to believe that their war was at the center of international policy and that their people were the heroes of the era.

Ho Chi Minh, a stubborn and complicated man, was still in complete control of North Vietnam's government. Nearly deified by his own people as "Uncle Ho," he was photographed with children and sitting at his simple desk, where he was depicted as directing a "people's war" against a technological superpower. However, Ho's army was more than a peasant soldier's; the sophisticated defense system he had built around Hanoi managed to bring down one plane in forty, and his armed forces were using tanks as well as surface-to-air missiles against the American aircraft. As his French biographer, Jean Lacouture, wrote: "Indeed, where does acting begin and end in the behavior of such a man? He is continually stage-managing himself, continually looking at situations with a producer's eye.... And yet, however 'artistic' he may be, a producer invariably expresses his inner temperament."

In the harsh propaganda published by North Vietnam, Ho Chi Minh denied that northern troops were fighting in the south, even though they had been sent there as early as 1960 and the United States had positive proof of their presence in 1962. Ho wanted to create an image of his people as grasshoppers fighting the elephant of "United States imperialism." To that end he demanded incredible patriotism and sacrifice from the North Vietnamese. The people had to "ensure, at any prices . . . victory on the 'great front' of the south." The north refused to publish its own casualty figures, in large part because the government did not want the people to know the heavy price they were paying.

It was as if time stood still in North Vietnam. Nothing mattered but winning this war, and life in Hanoi and the countryside remained stuck in the forties, when this war had begun. The people and their leaders were tied to the communism of the forties and the hardships brought on by the war. Ho Chi Minh kept to his self-imposed rule of writing little under his own name and giving few interviews to foreign journalists. When he was interviewed, he played the role of a wise Asian sage, not a communist leader who was willing to use every wile and to sacrifice every son of Vietnam to win. For instance, he told the British reporter Felix Greene how bitter he was that the Americans were escalating the war. "They say we want this war to go on. How can they say such a thing? You have seen the sufferings which the [bombing] raids have inflicted on our people. How can anyone want this dreadful war to continue? They leave us with no alternative but to fight on. We shall never give up our independence."

Greene suggested to Ho Chi Minh that North Vietnam should find a face-saving way to allow the Americans to withdraw with honor, to open a door so the United States could depart gracefully. Ho answered: "I know. I know. But you know, the door is open. They can leave at any time. . . . Once they have made up their minds, we shall do everything we can to help them. We'll even roll out the red carpet for them."

Soon afterward Ho told a French intermediary that for him there was no compromise regarding "the question of independence and honor," and he repeated his statement that negotiations with the United States would begin only when the bombing stopped. He wrote, "In the face of American aggression, our people are determined to fight, whatever the sacrifices, until final victory is achieved."

Not surprisingly, the communist Vietnamese began to see themselves as so menacing that even the world's greatest power could not stop them. Secret U.S. intelligence reports noted routinely and with mystification, that the American bombing was actually unifying the people of the north, not demoralizing them as was the intention. And on the Ho Chi

Minh Trail, tens of thousands of soldiers and workers marched south in an uninterrupted stream.

American officials were getting caught in a murderous battle of wills. Around the time that Ho's comments were published, a top American official told Jean Lacouture, "I admire Ho Chi Minh. . . . He's an engaging, even a fascinating figure. But he is not going to achieve his lifelong dream of uniting all Vietnam under his control. We have decided not to allow it. We will not let South Vietnam fall into his hands. I'm sorry for *his* sake, but that will never be."

As 1968 began, the American people were wondering whether they had the will to continue the Vietnam War and whether it was God's will that Americans die to prevent Ho Chi Minh from unifying Vietnam under communism. In January a South Carolina congressman put into the *Congressional Record* a moving letter from a father whose son had been killed in the war. "I cannot accept my son's death as a matter of God's will," the letter said. "I must reject a God who would create so well and then purposely destroy. The God I reverence is the God of creation. My son was destroyed, I am afraid, by me and by you and man's will, denying the will of God."

The American soldiers knew they were not headed toward victory, despite the claims of their superiors. Marine Captain Rodney R. Chastant wrote home that "morale is very high in spite of the fact that most men think the war is being run incorrectly. One of the staggering facts is that most men here believe we will *not* win the war. And yet they stick their necks out every day. . . . We must have more men, at least twice as many, or we are going to get the piss kicked out of us this winter when the rains come. . . . We should have never committed ourselves to this goal, but now that we have, what should we do?"

While that question was being mulled, the communists of the north and the south launched the Tet offensive on January 30 and 31, attacking almost one hundred cities and towns with a combined force of 67,000 troops against one million soldiers (nearly half of whom were Americans) defending the Saigon government.

The attack was not a complete surprise. On January 5 the U.S. military released a November 19, 1967, document captured by the CIA, which said that the communists were planning a "general offensive and general uprising" with particular orders that troops "should move toward liberating the capital city [of Saigon]." Neither the American press in Saigon nor the U.S. Army believed the document; it was considered propaganda to confuse them.

There were political and military reasons for doubting the communists' intentions and abilities. The American military command in Saigon had been reporting progress on the battlefield, which seemed to imply that the communists were growing weaker and were certainly not strong enough after the intensive U.S. bombing campaign to launch such an offensive. In late December the top American military officials sent a cable to Washington describing the communists' plan to "undertake an intensified countrywide effort" but said that this would take place outside the cities.

The attacks began shortly after midnight on Tuesday, January 30. This was the start of Tet, the lunar New Year holiday that is the most important festival for Vietnamese, when families get together to have feasts and exchange gifts.

The United States had agreed to a nationwide truce at that time, which the communist attacks violated. Six cities, including Da Nang, South Vietnam's second largest, were hit, replacing the happy sound of the traditional firecrackers with the loud noise of artillery fire. At dawn that morning the United States canceled the truce and began frantically preparing a defense against what it feared could be a much larger communist offensive.

Shortly before three the next morning, the communists attacked Saigon, including several military bases, the airport, the American Embassy, the presidential palace, and the government radio station. Some twenty communist commandos struck the embassy, using a taxi, a small truck, and explosives. They first tore a hole in the embassy's outside wall, then used a rocket launcher to blast the front doors of the Chancery Building. The few Americans inside immediately telephoned for help. Ambassador Ellsworth Bunker, at his residence nearby, called the South Vietnamese police. When the chief refused to send help, even though his headquarters was only one block away, Bunker ordered the American military police to rescue those in the embassy.

The American response was so confused that the invaders were able to stay inside the compound for hours, even though they were few in number and poorly organized. The Associated Press reported: "The Vietcong attacked Saigon Wednesday and seized part of the U.S. Embassy. American military police tried to storm in to the Embassy as dawn broke but were driven back by heavy outbursts of fire from the Embassy building." Another dispatch, at seven A.M., reported that the Vietnamese were still inside the embassy compound.

By ten A.M. the American military police had broken into the compound and a U.S. helicopter had landed on the roof. Nineteen Viet Cong solders were killed in the fighting. Later, the government backdated its repulse of the enemy and said the embassy had been declared officially "secure" at 9:15 that morning — but that was still six and a half hours after the first telephone call saying the embassy was under attack.

General Westmoreland explained this disaster to a group of journalists, largely Americans, saying, "The enemy's well-laid plans went afoul. Some superficial damage was done to the building. All of the enemy that entered the compound so far as I can determine were killed." According to *Washington Post* reporter Don Oberdorfer, "The reporters could hardly believe their ears. Westmoreland was standing in the ruins and saying everything was great."

Because of the twelve-hour time difference between Vietnam and the East Coast of the United States, the embassy attack occurred at the same time as the evening television news shows, and Americans heard about it immediately. During the first days of Tet the networks broadcast special programs, with such titles as "Vietcong Terror: A Guerrilla Offensive" and "Saigon Under Fire." The television coverage upset President Johnson and General Westmoreland even more than the newspaper articles. They tried to reverse the emphasis from a communist offensive to a communist defeat. It was true that the enemy was taking high casualties, but through the camera's viewfinder, it looked as if the communists had the initiative throughout the south.

This perception seemed to undermine all previous

claims by Johnson and the military that the Americans were making progress against the Vietnamese communists. The Tet offensive did reveal weaknesses in the Saigon army, the president and his commanding general conceded, but they still argued that there had been no "general uprising" against the Saigon government; in their estimation, Tet was a "complete failure" militarily.

This was a stunningly narrow definition, overlooking the fact that the war was as much about political victories as about military advances; Johnson and Westmoreland measured the Vietnamese offensive in terms of the ultimate goal of the communists — to create a popular uprising and an overthrow of the Saigon regime — rather than admit that by holding the U.S. Embassy for a few hours, the Viet Cong had demonstrated they were gaining momentum in the south. Senator Eugene McCarthy of Minnesota, who was challenging Johnson for the Democratic party's presidential nomination, said that the communists' "attacks on the cities of South Vietnam show that we don't have the country under any kind of control and that we are in a much worse position than we were in two years ago."

The Tet offensive targeted provincial capitals throughout the south, from Khe Sanh near the demilitarized zone down to Can Tho in the Mekong delta. They bombarded American bases as well as ARVN strongholds that were supposed to be impregnable. The south erupted in battle, but in most cases the American and ARVN forces were able to beat back the advances of the overstretched communists. However, the offensive contradicted American claims that the communists were in retreat; on the contrary, they were determined to fight to the finish.

Along with the invasion of the U.S. Embassy, which

was impressive as a symbol but not as a military operation, the Tet offensive is remembered for the great battle for the city of Hue. On January 31 the communists captured the beautiful former capital and flew the NLF flag over its citadel. They took control of every part of the city except the American compound and the South Vietnamese army camp on the southern bank of the Perfume River.

During their occupation of Hue, the North Vietnamese and Viet Cong reorganized the city and tried to bring its population under their sway. But the people of this city, known for their intense political passions, were not won over easily. Although few actually resisted, the majority did not welcome the communists with open arms. The communists went door to door looking for Vietnamese who worked for the Saigon government or the Americans and for foreigners who might be considered spies. They executed at least 1,000 and as many as 3,000 Vietnamese, Europeans, and Americans. The corpses, many with their hands still bound behind their backs, were thrown into mass graves.

Meanwhile American marines launched a counterassault to recapture Hue. They first attacked the southern bank of the river, then crossed it to recapture the imperial city and the citadel. The marines fought door to door and block to block to evict the communists. Sharpshooters aimed from second-story windows, firing down on fleeing shadows in the rubble of the old city's streets. Priceless treasures were blown away in the cross-fire and crushed underfoot by soldiers. While the marines and ARVN soldiers fought through to the citadel, the communists held on to the eastern quarter of the city. Then on February 24, three weeks after they entered Hue, the communists retreated, and the Americans and ARVN recaptured the entire city. Over 10,000 soldiers were reported killed during the battle for Hue. North Vietnamese rockets and American bombs and artillery fire destroyed entire neighborhoods of the city.

Upon recapturing Hue, the Americans found the mass graves of the people executed by the communists. Historian Stanley Karnow wrote that just after the communists fled, the Saigon army brought in commandos who assassinated Vietnamese accused of working with the communists during the occupation. These bodies, he wrote, were thrown "into common graves with the Vietcong's victims. The city's entire population suffered in one way or another from the ordeal."

President Johnson warned that the Hue massacre was a taste of what would happen if the communists won control of the whole country. Other observers who were sympathetic to the north and the NLF fired back that Hue was an exception. On balance, the Hue massacre revealed that the communists were capable of committing atrocities on a mass scale. Previously they had killed only those officials of the Saigon regime actively engaged in war against them. Executing thousands of people without trial was a far different crime. But the battle for Hue sadly underlined that the Saigon regime offered little alternative to any Vietnamese caught in the middle.

While American marines were fighting in the streets, houses, and alleys of Hue, the battle for Khe Sanh, farther north, tested them in classic open-field warfare. That battle began one week after the attack on Hue but lasted twice as long, nearly two months, and was extensively reported by

American television. Viewers saw a battle that brought to mind battles of the Second World War.

The American marines were surrounded by North Vietnamese infantry but were well protected by the air force, which dropped at least 70,000 tons of bombs on the enemy over a period of some nine weeks, setting a record at the time for intensive bombing. The casualty figures from the air assault were astonishing. The North Vietnamese reportedly lost 10,000 soldiers; the marines only 500. The deadly air war strategy worked at Khe Sanh, and the Americans held off the North Vietnamese.

The victory at Khe Sanh and in the Tet offensive as a whole, however, was controversial. General Westmoreland was criticized for failing to predict the massive assault on the south. Moreover, a significant number of South Vietnamese had known about the communists' plans months in advance but had betrayed nothing and in some cases had helped the enemy. Why, the American public asked, did they not help the government? Whose side were they on? This led back to the basic question of how long the United States could continue propping up a regime that was incapable of or uninterested in mobilizing the South Vietnamese to defend themselves against the north. The communists may not have scored a major battlefield victory in Tet, but they won a political victory beyond their imagination by sowing grave doubts in the minds of the American public.

In the aftermath of Tet, the respected television journalist Walter Cronkite went to Vietnam and reported, "It seems now more certain than ever that the bloody experience of Vietnam is to end in a stalemate. . . . The only rational way out then will be to negotiate, not as victors but as an honorable people who lived up to their pledge to defend democracy, and did the best they could."

The Tet offensive also gave the war its darkest quotation. An American major who escorted the press corps around the Mekong delta town of Ben Tre explained that the heavy damage by helicopter fire was unavoidable in the effort to rout the Viet Cong. He said, "It became necessary to destroy the town to save it."

In April 1968 one million students across the United States boycotted classes in a national student strike against the war. That same month, opinion polls registered that nearly half of the American people now believed the war in Vietnam was a mistake.

The Backdrop of Destruction

The major's view that U.S. soldiers had to destroy a village to save it shocked the American public. Scientists had already asked Johnson to examine the effect this modern war, with its intensive bombing, napalm, and herbicides, was having on Vietnam's long-term survival. In February 1967 five thousand scientists, including seventeen Nobel Prize winners, had signed a petition demanding that the president immediately end the spraying of herbicides on Vietnam and review America's policy regarding chemical and biological warfare. Johnson did not reply.

The use of herbicides was the practice that most upset the scientists. In 1962 the United States sprayed 5,600 acres in the south with the herbicides Agent Orange, Agent White, and Agent Blue; in 1967, with U.S. troops actively fighting the war, 1,707,700 acres were sprayed, bringing the total to nearly 3 million acres. The purpose was to destroy the jungles where the communists hid and the croplands where they grew their food.

However, the Americans had difficulty distinguishing between civilian friends and foes. The majority of the ruined croplands and riverbeds had provided food for friendly Vietnamese, not the enemy. For instance, in 1967 farmers in Long Khanh province gave the American adviser in their district a petition that read, "We are people who live by farming alone and have fallen into a deficient, indigent situation because of the influence of defoliation. The American military performed this by planes spreading chemicals and the effect . . . has made various types of fruit trees lose their leaves, ruined fruit, and [made] crops such as green beans, white beans, peanuts, soybeans and black beans lose their leaves, then die. . . . We sincerely request you suggest that the higher authorities send personnel to inspect the crops affected in order to compensate for our losses."

But the spraying continued, and American soldiers began to suspect that these herbicides were affecting them also. Questions about Agent Orange as a cause of cancer, sterility, and birth defects in infants born to the wives of Vietnam veterans are still being studied.

Scientists were also concerned that the bombing and use of herbicides and the massive destruction of the countryside would affect the ecological balance. Malaria and bubonic plague were two often-cited results of the war. In 1961 Vietnam reported only eight cases of plague, but by the end of 1967, after hundreds of thousands of Vietnamese had been uprooted and sent to dirty refugee camps, plague flourished. Approximately 5,500 cases were reported, resulting in 350 deaths. Malaria was spread by mosquitoes, which used water-filled bomb craters as breeding grounds. Tuberculosis, leprosy, dysentery, typhoid fever, and venereal disease all spread with alarming speed in this country of dislocated families and disrupted or nonexistent health care.

The U.S. military's use of napalm caused the greatest outcry in the United States. When dropped in bombs or hurled in flame throwers, napalm sets fire to anything it touches and releases a nauseous black cloud. The effect on the human body is almost too painful to describe. The explosion of a napalm bomb makes a person's stomach turn and sharply stings the eyes. When the burning jelly touches human skin, the damage is devastating. A French doctor who examined some of its victims in North Vietnam said, "Inside the wound or burn, it burns slowly. On occasion this slow combustion lasts up to fifteen days. At night, the greenish light produced by the material can be seen as it continues burning the flesh and bones."

In January 1967 the *Ladies Home Journal* published pictures of young victims of napalm, their skin seeming to have melted, their wounds bleeding like giant cysts. These children's stories upset the leaders in Washington as much as the now routinely critical reporting in the national press because they raised disturbing moral questions for the average American family.

It became clear that this war had two battle fronts, one in Vietnam and the other in the United States. In Vietnam the president had to show the North Vietnamese and the Viet Cong that they could not take over the south. At home he had to convince the American public that the war was worth the financial costs, the risk of rising inflation, and, above all else, the lives of their sons and brothers.

Johnson was losing on both battle fronts.

Turning Point

Even though the United States had successfully defeated the Tet offensive, the American public felt that it had destroyed any hope that the war would be over soon. Many Americans were now less concerned about winning the war than about getting out of Vietnam; the price had become too high. Johnson and Westmoreland felt that the media had misled the public by failing to emphasize sufficiently the losses suffered by the communists.

Still the president pressed on with his war effort. Privately Westmoreland asked Johnson for an additional 206,000 American troops to be sent to Vietnam. On March 1, 1968, Johnson asked his new secretary of defense, Clark Clifford, to evaluate the request. Clifford gathered a task force to write a report for the president, but the group was divided. The report said Johnson should do what he wished about sending troops, but later Clifford said of his investigation: "I could not find out when the war was going to end; I could not find out the manner in which it was going to end; I could not find out whether the new requests for men and equipment were going to be enough, or whether it would take more and, if more, when and how much; I could not find out how soon the South Vietnamese forces would be ready to take over. All I had was the statement given with too little self-assurance to be comforting, that if we persisted for an indeterminate length of time, the enemy would choose not to go on."

Members of Congress told the president's advisers that sending more American soldiers to Vietnam was a mistake. Even supporters of the war, such as Senator Henry M. Jackson of Washington, said Vietnam was becoming a "bottom-less pit." Secretary of State Dean Rusk began arguing for a halt to the bombing of North Vietnam; he also wanted new diplomatic proposals that would convince the Hanoi government to negotiate with the United States.

News of Westmoreland's secret request for 206,000 additional troops became public when the *New York Times* ran a story on March 10, 1968, about the debates within the government. The president was angry that the story had been leaked, and the public was angry that more troops had been requested. Two days later, in the New Hampshire primary, the first to be held in the race for the presidential nomination, Senator Eugene McCarthy, who was running an antiwar campaign, won 42 percent of the Democratic vote. He received only 330 votes fewer than Johnson. Four days later, on March 16, Senator Robert F. Kennedy of New York, brother of the assassinated former president, announced that he too would challenge Johnson for the Democratic nomination. Johnson's campaign managers feared the president might actually lose the next primary, in Wisconsin.

The day before, on March 15, Johnson had received another confidential report on the war, written by Dean Acheson, who had been secretary of state during the Truman administration. Johnson had asked Acheson, one of the country's most respected statesmen, to review American policy in Vietnam and advise him. Acheson had asked officials at all levels in all the relevant departments for briefings on the military and political situation. He concluded that the Tet offensive had proven the American force was far too small to get rid of the North Vietnamese in the south and to destroy the Viet Cong. It would take at least five more years and far more soldiers and money than the American public would tolerate. In a word, Acheson said, the war had become hopeless.

Pressured now from all sides, Johnson first told Westmoreland through the Joint Chiefs of Staff that it would be impossible to send 206,000 additional troops. Only 13,500 new troops would be added to the American forces. Then on March 23 the president announced that Westmoreland would be transferred out of Vietnam. Johnson could no longer believe Westmoreland's optimistic scenarios; he had lost faith in the strategy of escalating American involvement.

After Westmoreland's transfer, Johnson searched for a new strategy. On March 25 he met with Acheson and several other former officials whom he called the "wise old men," a group he had brought together four months earlier to discuss the war. At that time they had endorsed his policy. Now Johnson asked the wise men to meet in secret that evening with the officials responsible for the conduct of the war. When one of the wise men asked how long it would take to get the North Vietnamese out of the south and "pacify" the countryside, he was told, "Maybe five years, maybe ten years." The group was astonished; when they had asked that question at their earlier meeting, the answer had been as little as one year.

After the meetings, the group presented their opinion to the president. Most said the United States could not win the war with the time and resources that the American people would tolerate. Acheson could not see how the South Vietnamese government could ever support or defend itself. He told Johnson that the United States would never be able to provide what was most needed, popular support for the Saigon regime.

On March 31 Johnson addressed the nation. He talked about Vietnam and what he wanted to achieve through the war. He said the suffering continued, but he blamed Hanoi. Then the president made a public gesture toward peace. "We are prepared to move immediately toward peace through negotiations. . . . Tonight, I have ordered our aircraft and our naval vessels to make no attacks on North Vietnam, except in . . . the demilitarized zone." This was the unilateral bombing halt Hanoi had insisted on before it would go ahead with negotiations. "There is no need to delay talks that could bring an end to this long and this bloody war," Johnson said.

Johnson had more surprises. He ended his speech with expressions of concern about the sacrifices Americans were making in Vietnam and about the political divisions it was creating at home. "With America's sons in the fields far away, with America's future under challenge right here at home . . . I do not believe that I should devote an hour or a day of my time to any personal partisan causes." Then he shocked the nation and the world. "Accordingly, I shall not seek, and I will not accept, the nomination of my party for another term as your president."

The aftershocks of the Tet offensive led Johnson to give up the race for president and confirmed suspicions that had been growing in the minds of the American public for the past two years. Within three days Hanoi accepted the president's offer, and plans began for peace talks in Paris.

Because he had been a strong champion for a negotiated settlement to the war, Defense Secretary Clifford began devising a way for the United States to leave Vietnam honorably. He scheduled the first conference for May 10, in Paris, and told the American delegation to come up with a solution, perhaps before the presidential election in November.

But like a Greek tragedy, America's war in Vietnam had become too charged with conceits about honor and about saving the world for democracy to end in anything but sadness and even terror. The Vietnamese communists were afflicted with the same pride, although it was manifested differently. They possessed an inflexible sense of mission to save Vietnam's national identity and to win complete freedom from foreign control. Both sides wanted to be heroes if not winners.

So instead of marking an end to the agony, the peace negotiations actually represented a midway point in the war, separating one phase from another.

Days of Rage

The year 1968 proved to be a momentous one in the United States, marked by two assassinations that profoundly affected the country.

Dr. Martin Luther King, Jr. was already considered a great hero when he began to speak out against the war, becoming one of the most effective and respected leaders of the antiwar movement. On April 4, 1968, King was assassinated at a motel in Memphis, Tennessee. Immediately, angry blacks rioted in the streets of America's cities. Ghettos in 110 cities across the nation were set aflame in riots that left 39 people dead and another 2,500 injured. King was the spiritual leader, the symbol of black nonviolent protest against racism, segregation, and injustice. The black community had lost its most respected leader, and few people believed that only one man was responsible. Many young people, minorities, and activists committed to King, as well as some of the general public, believed there was a conspiracy of powerful people behind James Earl Ray, the lone gunman charged with King's murder.

Robert F. Kennedy was another leading figure against the war. As early as March 1967, as a senator from New York, he spoke out against the country's involvement in Vietnam. In a speech calling for "negotiations now," he told the Senate that as an adviser to his brother, President John F. Kennedy, he had played a role in the decisions that led the United States into the war. Even though he was only attorney general and therefore not directly responsible for those decisions, he told the Senate, "I can testify that if fault is to be found or responsibility assessed, there is enough to go around for all — including myself."

Kennedy was the only top official who had admitted publicly that he had made a mistake about Vietnam. "We are not in Vietnam to play the role of an avenging angel pouring death and destruction on the roads and factories and homes of a guilty land," he said. Pleading for negotiations, Kennedy said, "Can anyone believe this nation, with all its fantastic power and resources, will be endangered by a wise and magnanimous action toward a small and difficult adversary?"

Late in the race for the Democratic presidential nomination, Kennedy entered with a strong antiwar campaign. He wanted to do away with draft deferments that allowed those young men who could afford college to avoid the war. His solution was a universal draft determined by lottery. This, he felt, would end the hypocrisy of American leaders who promoted the war but kept their sons out of the fighting through draft deferments.

Indeed, Kennedy made inequality his campaign theme, denouncing a society that "spends twice as much on pets as on the poverty program." Media expert Marshall McLuhan said that during his campaign Kennedy created an "easy rapport with the surging generosity of young hearts" and called him a "reluctant hero." The respected journalist Joseph Alsop, who backed the war, said that what came through in Kennedy's speeches was "a sense of deep and true concern, a feeling that this man genuinely cares very greatly."

Kennedy had enemies. Many liberals believed he had been too ruthless in the past, making deals and failing to keep promises, and could not be trusted. On the other extreme, some conservatives were convinced he was a communist. But Kennedy was taking on a mythical stature, inheriting his brother's legacy and convincing the downtrodden, especially blacks, that he would be a fair president. By early summer he was running a close second to Vice President Hubert Humphrey, who entered the race after Johnson withdrew. Humphrey was the favorite of the traditional leaders of the party, the segment known as the "establishment" in those days, while Kennedy was the candidate of the young.

On June 5, the night he won the California primary and appeared poised to win the nomination itself, Robert F. Kennedy was assassinated in Los Angeles. With Kennedy's death, the antiwar movement lost the only presidential candidate who could win and who was trusted to end the war. His assassination, on the heels of King's two months earlier, broke the last slender ties between the traditional leaders of the Democratic party and the young, the liberal, the dispossessed, and the angry.

Again, there were doubts that Kennedy's assassin, Sirhan Sirhan, could figure out by himself how to murder Kennedy and then get close enough to fire his gun without assistance from others. Grief over the deaths of King and Kennedy was complicated by the fear that the assassinations were politically motivated and had been covered up to protect powerful people. These suspicions inflamed the country further.

The extreme left of the antiwar movement had no love for Kennedy and were stingy in their praise of the nonviolence practiced by King, but movement historian Todd Gitlin believes that even this group was undone by the assassinations, by what Gitlin calls "the murder of hope." Violence spawned more violence, and thereafter the far left broke away from mainstream America over the war.

The antiwar movement adopted more radical and even violent tactics. If the U.S. government could use police to break up their marches, they felt they could break a few minor laws to make the government uncomfortable until the war ended. The police and the Federal Bureau of Investigation (FBI) were tapping the phones of people in the antiwar movement, and the CIA joined in secret surveillance operations. The police and FBI sent undercover agents to movement meetings and used the information they gained to disrupt planned demonstrations or to provoke demonstrators to break laws. Once the demonstrators realized that they were being infiltrated and manipulated, new fear and paranoia settled over the movement. In a demonstration in Oakland, California, staged to close down a draft induction office, the demonstrators, realizing that the police had been tipped off to their plans, fought back when the police tried to clear them away. Demonstrators burned draft cards, blocked traffic, damaged some cars, and made a general nuisance of themselves, then escaped when it looked like they might be arrested. Violence, as one leader said, was becoming "as American as apple pie."

All of this seemed to mirror the violence in the Vietnam War. That war was coming home to America, and the biggest battle was at the August convention of the Democratic party in Chicago. Various groups in the antiwar movement had planned demonstrations months in advance of the Chicago convention. The three main groups, including the National Mobilization to End the War in Vietnam, asked for parade permits for their demonstrations, but the city and the groups could not agree where, when, or how the demonstrations would be held. Many in the National Mobilization believed that the American system of government was at fault for the war and that the only way to end it was to demonstrate in the streets. The group known as the Yippies, on the other hand, wanted to proclaim their opposition to the entire society and to celebrate, as they put it, a counterculture advocating drugs, sex, and rock music. As one of their leaders said, "Freedom is the right to stand on the streetcorner and do nothing. . . . [Long hair] is a symbol of rejection of the old order . . . the military, careers, university bullshit, outmoded mores and split-level living."

Chicago's Mayor Richard Daley, a Democrat, was one of the last of the big-city mayors who ran his city like a small fiefdom. Keeping his pledge to prevent the antiwar protestors from disrupting the convention, he set up a security system that included 12,000 police and 6,000 National Guardsmen patrolling the streets. Delegates to the convention had to pass through at least six security checkpoints. Chicago looked like a war zone.

On Wednesday, August 28, the pent-up anger of the police and the outrage of the demonstrators led to violence. Kept away from the convention delegates they wanted to influence, the demonstrators broke through the police barriers and began a march toward the Hilton Hotel, where many delegates were staying. After a half hour the police attacked them with tear gas, Mace (a stinging chemical sprayed from a can), and clubs, injuring innocent bystanders as well as reporters covering the convention. Later a special report by the National Commission on Violence, based on 20,000 pages of eyewitness statements, film, and photographs, said that although taunted by the demonstrators, the police *had* rioted and had been "unrestrained and indiscriminate." Before the convention ended, the respected Senator Abraham Ribicoff of Connecticut criticized Mayor Daley's "Gestapo tactics in the streets of Chicago," and the Colorado delegation asked if "Mayor Daley can be compelled to suspend the police state terror."

The events surrounding the Chicago convention became a turning point for American politics. The antiwar groups declared that what happened at the convention was a sign there was "no turning back" and cut themselves off from the more moderate liberal Democrats.

At the convention itself, the delegates rejected a "peace plank" that called for an unconditional end to the bombing of North Vietnam and for the negotiation of a mutual withdrawal from South Vietnam by the United States and North Vietnamese groups. The Democrats nominated Humphrey as their presidential candidate, which in effect was a vote in support of Johnson's handling of the war.

Humphrey campaigned on a platform of peace, but he never specified how he would bring about America's withdrawal from Southeast Asia. Governor George Wallace of Alabama, a former Democrat, ran on a third-party ticket. His running mate was a former chief of the air force, who advocated nuclear attacks against North Vietnam if necessary. The Republican candidate, Richard M. Nixon, said early on in the campaign that he had a secret plan to bring the war to an end.

The liberals were lukewarm in their support for Humphrey, and the left, which rejected all of the men running for president, routinely heckled the Democratic candidate. They doubted that any of the candidates would end the war.

In the general election that November, both Humphrey and Nixon won 43 percent of the popular vote, with Wallace picking up the rest. Some analysts said the margin was so narrow in some states that Humphrey could have won if the left wing of the Democratic party had all voted for him. But Nixon won handily in the electoral college, carrying thirty-two states to Humphrey's thirteen and the District of Columbia. Americans had voted for what they perceived as a solid law and order Republican candidate who also promised peace in Vietnam. After a year that had brought the Tet offensive, two assassinations, inner-city riots following the King murder, and the Chicago convention, the public wanted an end to the war and to the strife at home.

With the election of Nixon, Americans thought their war in Vietnam would soon be over and the divisions in their communities healed.

7

DYING TO SAVE FACE,

1969–1975

Richard M. Nixon did not have a new, secret plan to end America's war in Vietnam. Instead he had strategies for putting greater pressure on North Vietnam to leave the south. His military strategy required expanding the war to other countries in order to end America's involvement; he may have called this strategy by another name, but it was essentially the old idea of escalation. Above all else, however, Nixon's mission was to not be "the first president of the United States to lose a war."

Nixon wanted to leave Vietnam in a way that did not require victory but would not appear to be an American defeat. This had been Lyndon Johnson's goal as early as January 1966, when McNamara's aide wrote, "The present U.S. objective in Vietnam is to avoid humiliation. The reasons why we *went into* Vietnam to the present depth are

166

varied; but they are now largely academic." Johnson's presidency crumbled while he tried to save face in Vietnam, and Nixon's new Republican team was continuing the fighting for much the same reason, to find an "honorable peace" that would allow Nixon to say he had not lost the war.

The president and his national security adviser, Henry M. Kissinger, continued the talks in Paris with the Vietnamese communists, but in a different spirit from Johnson and without the same battle scars. Nixon and Kissinger, discarding the lessons learned by previous administrations, were guided by the old illusion that the Saigon regime could become a strong, independent democracy if given a few more years of aid from the United States. But even with a half million U.S. troops at their side, the South Vietnamese army could not drive out the communists; indeed, intelligence reports showed considerable support for the communists throughout the southern countryside. The Saigon government continued to lose legitimacy.

In search of an honorable retreat, the Republicans were walking down a blind alley. For twenty-five years before Nixon took office, the Vietnamese communists had been fighting to unify Vietnam. Nixon had no reason to believe they would change their goals because he was president. Once the U.S. withdrew, the war would continue until the country was unified. There was no question that the North Vietnamese had the stronger fighting force.

Back in the War Zone

By 1968 American casualties had risen to 15,000, 60 percent of those in 1967. Being told that they were fighting and dying for democracy in Vietnam was hard enough for American GIs to accept, but it was utterly dispiriting to be told they were risking their lives for an "honorable peace." They were not certain what that meant, but it was vague enough to cause deep concern.

Not surprisingly, the statistics for drug use by American soldiers climbed dramatically during the Nixon years. According to a Department of Defense survey, by 1971 half of the GIs in Vietnam smoked marijuana; 13 percent said they smoked grass daily. The same survey said that nearly 10 percent used opium or its derivative heroin daily. These drugs were easily available: marijuana was grown in Vietnam, and opium could be gotten easily from the nearby fields of the "golden triangle," which includes Laos, Thailand, and Burma. The narcotic addictions that the GIs developed in Vietnam they brought back home with them. Ninety-three percent of the soldiers who used heroin said they had never tried it before they were drafted. The highest rate of drug use was near the front lines; another army survey showed that "more persons in combat units use marijuana than in other units."

Soldiers who were so demoralized that they smoked marijuana and used hard drugs were unenthusiastic about fighting the war. The question "What are you fighting for?" was not just a clever saying among the GIs but a profound puzzle. The rates of desertion and absences without leave in the army jumped 400 percent, from less than 15 per 1,000 in 1966 to 73 per 1,000 in 1971. Army desertion and AWOL rates in 1971 were the highest recorded in modern American history — 7 desertions and 17 AWOLs for every 100 soldiers, according to military historian David Cortright in *Soldiers in Revolt*. The Vietnam War desertion rate was three times higher than that in the Korean War and higher than the previous record during the Second World War of 63 per 1,000. The reasons for the desertions were different this time. In Vietnam the "servicemen took off not because of danger but because of disgust," according to Cortright.

In August 1969 the *New York Daily News* published the first reported incident of mass mutiny in Vietnam. Two days earlier, sixty exhausted soldiers had refused to continue a campaign south of Da Nang after five days of fighting and many casualties. In November another mutiny was reported near the Cambodian border. And in April 1970 a CBS television crew filmed a group of soldiers as they told their captain that his order was nonsense and they would not obey him.

This first year of Nixon's command of the Vietnam War also brought news of the My Lai massacre, which had taken place in 1968, not long after Tet. At least two hundred Vietnamese civilians of the village of My Lai in the central South Vietnamese province of Quang Ngai had been murdered by American troops in a sort of rampage. According to the official reports after the incident was investigated, Lieutenant W. L. Calley led his platoon of thirty men into My Lai and ordered them to assault the people with gunfire and throw grenades into the huts even though the Americans were not facing opposing fire. The inhabitants, mainly women, children, and old men, were killed as they held their hands above their heads or after being shepherded to a ditch. The massacre was not reported to Washington, but a soldier-journalist named Ronald Ridenhour tracked down numerous rumors about it until the story came out in late 1969.

The My Lai revelations opened a Pandora's box of questions about the effect of a war like Vietnam on the soldiers called upon to fight. As a U.S. Marine medic was quoted by Canadian journalist Michael Maclear in *The Ten Thousand Day War*, "It was taught to us, go into this Ville [village], and you have to blow everything away in this Ville. Your basic mistrust of the Vietnamese people is already ingrained in you: anything with slant eyes was a 'gook' — they were not human beings."

Another strand in the unraveling of American military morale was the bitter revolt of black soldiers against what they saw as racism in the military. Even before Nixon's election there were stories of black riots in Vietnam. Blacks throughout the battle area reacted in anger when they heard about King's assassination in the spring of 1968. "The death of Martin Luther King intruded on the war in a way that no other outside event had ever done," wrote Michael Herr in his classic book *Dispatches*. "In the days that followed, there were a number of small, scattered riots, one or two stabbings, all of it denied officially. The Marine recreational facility in China Beach in Danang was put off-limits for a day, and at Stud we stood around the radio and listened to the sound of automatic weapons fire being broadcast from a number of American cities."

Later Herr had a drink with a black staff sergeant from Alabama, who asked rhetorically, "Now what I gonna do? . . . Am I gonna take 'n' turn them guns aroun' on my own people?" Nearly all the black noncommissioned officers Herr talked to that day were asking the same question. As one sergeant was leaving, he said, "Oh, man. This war gets old."

In 1970 fighting broke out between black and white American soldiers near the front lines; in 1971 a black soldier was killed in a racial clash near the DMZ, and nearly 200 black soldiers went to his funeral to protest racism in the army.

Both black and white soldiers began "fragging," or injuring — in some cases even killing — commanding officers to avoid going into combat. In 1971 Congress held hearings on fragging, and Republican Senator Charles Mathias of Maryland said: "In every war a new vocabulary springs up. . . . But in all the lexicon of war there is not a more tragic word than fragging, with all that it implies of total failure of discipline and depression of morale, the complete sense of frustration and confusion and the loss of goals and hope itself."

Many politicians were appalled at what the army described as assaults by U.S. soldiers on their officers using explosive devices. In 1969 and 1970, 300 incidents were reported that caused 73 deaths and almost 500 injuries. Articles about fragging in newspapers and magazines created the impression that the army was fighting a war within a war. One former marine colonel wrote in the June 1971 *Armed Forces Journal*, "The morale, discipline and battleworthiness of the U.S. armed forces are, with a few salient exceptions, lower and worse than at any time in this century and possibly in the history of the United States."

The Nixon-Kissinger Strategy

While these quasi-mutinies were occurring, the soldiers had embarked on Nixon and Kissinger's new military strategy. In

March 1969 the president secretly approved the military's long-standing request to bomb the Vietnamese communists' sanctuaries just over the border in neighboring Cambodia. The bombing lasted fourteen months with the goal of destroying the communists' supply routes and rear base support. American planes were bombing the sovereign independent country of Cambodia without its permission and without even warning the country itself. Many people doubted that this was legal, but neither the Cambodian government nor the Vietnamese communists protested. Cambodia was pretending to be neutral in the war, even though its leader, Prince Norodom Sihanouk, had given the Vietnamese communists permission to use the border area and had allowed their supplies to be shipped through the Cambodian seaport of Sihanoukville and then overland. Any protests on his part could have made clear that his country was in fact not neutral.

The bombing of Cambodia might have remained a secret if the *New York Times* Pentagon reporter, William Beecher, had not tracked down the story and published it in May 1969. Beecher reported that the bombings were intended to demonstrate that the new administration was "tougher" than Johnson had been, willing to punish Hanoi militarily while negotiating in Paris. The White House denied the accounts, and both Nixon and Kissinger were upset by the story, which they believed had been leaked by a top Pentagon official. When Kissinger asked FBI Director J. Edgar Hoover to find out how the reporter had learned about the secret bombings, the FBI put wiretaps on several people's telephones without following the proper legal procedure. The administration continued the secret bombing, dropping more than 100,000 tons of explosives on Cambodia.

That year Nixon agreed to token reductions in the number of American troops in Vietnam as part of the peace plan presented to the communists at the talks in Paris. But neither the communists nor the U.S. commander in South Vietnam, General Creighton W. Abrams, was happy with the reductions. Abrams was overseeing the "Vietnamization" of the war, begun under Johnson, which was meant to prepare ARVN to fight the communists on their own. As historian George C. Herring wrote in *America's Longest War*, even the "crash programs" of 1968 to improve ARVN's performance and attack the Viet Cong infrastructure "did not decisively alter the military or political balance in South Vietnam." The Saigon regime made some gains, but "the stalemate persisted." Abrams felt that American troops should not be withdrawn until Vietnamization had been given a chance.

Nixon's withdrawal failed to impress the communists, either. They called it a "farce" and refused to budge on their demands that all U.S. forces be withdrawn from Vietnam and that a provisional coalition government be created that did not include Thieu, who was still the head of the Saigon regime. At home the antiwar movement was very suspicious of Nixon's intentions and on October 15, 1969, organized a national "moratorium" involving several million people who held peaceful vigils in churches, marched in candlelight parades, and held antiwar petition drives. This demonstrated to the White House that the antiwar sentiment was now shared by a large and respectable segment of the population. Another moratorium was held on November 15.

Unbeknownst to the protestors, their solemn and convincing demonstrations caused Nixon to cancel an earlier secret plan to bomb the north and mine its rivers and harbors. Later Nixon admitted that "after all the protests and the Moratorium, American public opinion would be seriously divided by a military escalation of the war."

Expanding the War

On March 18, 1970, the Cambodian legislature met and voted unanimously to withdraw its confidence in the chief of state, Prince Sihanouk. This has been called a coup de chef d'état, the overthrow of the head of government but not the government itself. There are doubts that this vote was legal, but no doubt that it was important.

The new leaders of Cambodia rejected Prince Sihanouk's policy of allowing the Vietnamese communists to use their country in the war against the Saigon government. The new regime believed Sihanouk had threatened Cambodia's independence by giving up too much to the Vietnamese communists. When they ordered the communists to leave Cambodian territory, the Vietnamese replied that they did not recognize this new government; to them Prince Sihanouk remained the legitimate leader of Cambodia, and he had not asked them to evacuate their sanctuaries along the Cambodian-Vietnamese border.

A whole new chapter of the Vietnam War began. The new leaders of Cambodia, headed by General Lon Nol, asked the United States for help against the Vietnamese, opening the door to legitimate American attacks against the communists' sanctuaries. It was the request the Americans had been waiting for.

Since the Tet offensive, far fewer guerrilla groups had been operating in the south. The war was turning into a more conventional military conflict in which winning territory and gaining control of the country were the goals. It was becoming clear that the North Vietnamese now controlled the communist movement in the south; the Viet Cong had been badly damaged in the Tet Offensive and had become entirely subordinate to the northerners. The determination of the North Vietnamese to win stood in sharp contrast to the Saigon army's refusal to sacrifice and fight to hold onto its own territory. Repeatedly, American troops would capture an area, in the process losing lives, and then retreat, leaving the encampment in the hands of the Saigon army. The communists would attack, and the Saigon army would retreat and abandon the territory to the communists. The Americans complained bitterly that they were winning the battles but losing the war.

By the spring of 1970, when Cambodia's new leaders decided to get the Vietnamese communists out of their country, the Saigon army faced a losing situation. As Stanley Karnow wrote, "From every indication, the Saigon regime would crumble if the Americans quit South Vietnam." A dramatic tactical move was required to keep the United States in the war until Nixon could find what he considered an honorable way out. Cambodia provided a new front where the American army could weaken the Vietnamese communists without having to meet them head on.

The Cambodian attempt to kick out the Vietnamese was doomed from the start. The North Vietnamese forces had no trouble defeating the meager Cambodian army. Prince Sihanouk joined sides with the Vietnamese communists and with his old enemies the Cambodian communists, known as the Khmer Rouge. Sihanouk, who considered himself the legitimate ruler of Cambodia, gave both groups permission to fight in his name to "liberate" the country. Within one month after taking office, the new Cambodian leader, Lon Nol, publicly appealed to all countries for help against Sihanouk and his communist allies.

On April 20 Nixon announced that 150,000 U.S. soldiers would be withdrawn from Southeast Asia within a year and said fatefully, "We finally have in sight the just peace we are seeking." Ten days later the United States answered Lon Nol's plea but without first warning the Cambodians. Together with ARVN, American troops launched a full-scale surprise attack against the Vietnamese communists' military headquarters in eastern Cambodia. Because Lon Nol had not been notified, the fighting was not coordinated with his army. And the Vietnamese communists had already withdrawn.

The Cambodian invasion had the same effect on American public opinion as the Tet offensive had had two years earlier. Sounding more strident than Johnson ever had, Nixon appeared on television to announce the Cambodian invasion. He said he had ordered it because he did not want to see "America become a second-rate power." He had been persuaded by the military officials that a campaign against the communists' sanctuaries in Cambodia would "buy time" for Vietnamization, allowing ARVN to strengthen its hold on the south and letting the United States withdraw without appearing to lose the war or desert its ally.

This time the public protests were louder and angrier than those following Tet. Within the government, four of Kissinger's aides resigned, and the secretary of the interior,

Walter Hickel, publicly protested the invasion. He was later fired, and two hundred State Department employees signed a protest. Newspapers from the *New York Times* to the *Wall Street Journal* criticized the invasion. College campuses erupted. Within five days of Nixon's announcement, a hundred student strikes were held across the country. On May 2 students at Yale University organized a national student strike. Polls showed a radical increase in student opposition to American involvement in Vietnam. Sixty-nine percent now called themselves "doves," or proponents of peace, and more than 40 percent believed that "the war in Vietnam is pure imperialism."

After the invasion of Cambodia, students closed down campuses. At some colleges, they burned the buildings that housed the Reserve Officer Training Corps (ROTC), where male students were trained for the military. When protesters at Kent State University in Ohio burned their ROTC building, Ohio governor James Rhodes ordered the National Guardsmen to go onto the campus and stop the protests. Rhodes said the protesters were "worse than the brownshirts" (as the Nazis were known) and said he would "eradicate" them. Nixon was also angry at the students, millions of whom were staging protests across the country, and called them "bums."

On May 4 the guardsmen sent to the Kent State campus fired into a crowd of students with real ammunition, not the dummy bullets often used to stop demonstrations. In the spasm of gunfire, four students were killed and nine were injured. They had simply been exercising their basic right of nonviolent freedom of speech and assembly.

The event caused the campuses to explode as never

before in American history. Seventy-five colleges remained closed for the entire year, and close to a million students demonstrated who had never taken part in a protest in their lives. They joined millions of other citizens who could not believe that America's Vietnam War, which the president had promised to end, was being expanded into Cambodia and that students could be killed for speaking out. Strikes were held at a third of the nation's colleges, and over half of the students on the country's 2,500 campuses took part.

Unlike Johnson, Nixon did not seem to care that the war was further dividing the nation. He told his White House staff, "Don't worry about divisiveness. Having drawn the sword, don't take it out — stick it in hard. . . . No defensiveness."

Cambodia and "Peace"

The Cambodian invasion did not significantly weaken the North Vietnamese communists. The U.S. troops failed to find their secret military headquarters; instead, they got embroiled in a new war. Although American combat troops left Cambodia that June, the United States spent close to $3 billion to underwrite the Lon Nol government and its war, and more than half a million tons of bombs were dropped on Cambodia during the Nixon presidency. The American strategy in Cambodia was to support Lon Nol against the communists insofar as that effort would help the United States end its war in Vietnam. But Lon Nol wanted to believe that the Americans had given him an open-ended commitment to fight communism in his country, so the two countries were working at cross-purposes. The United

States encouraged Lon Nol's misperception of its largesse and watched as his government grew corrupt on American aid and his army became too weak to fight.

In addition, the United States had entered the war in Laos, the third country of Indochina. The communists there were true protégés of the Vietnamese communists and had waged an insurgency against the government in the capital of Vientiane according to orders from Hanoi. From the 1960s through 1975, the U.S. spent $2.5 billion in Laos, and in ten years of an air war dropped over two million tons of bombs on Laos. But, as in Cambodia, widening the war into Laos failed to weaken the North Vietnamese.

The greatest disappointment for Nixon was the failure of either his Cambodian invasion or the Laos campaign to budge the North Vietnamese at the bargaining table in Paris, where two sets of negotiations were under way. One was the public peace talks, with all the Vietnamese parties represented: the North Vietnamese, the Viet Cong, and the South Vietnamese government. The other negotiations, which were secret, had begun in a suburb of Paris in 1969 between Henry Kissinger and Le Duc Tho, a top official of the Hanoi government. These talks were kept secret from Saigon as long as possible because they represented all too starkly where the power lay and who would decide how the war would end. Little came of the discussions in the first year because of the death of Ho Chi Minh. With their leader gone, the North Vietnamese seemed more firmly entrenched in their old negotiating positions.

Nixon set up a special presidential commission late in the summer of 1970 to study the effect the war was having on American students and the broader society. He named former Republican governor William Scranton of Pennsylvania as its chairman. The commission's findings were disturbing. Scranton reported that the United States was more deeply divided than at any time since the Civil War and that it was essential that America's Vietnam War come to an end. The president had to react. In October he announced he would seek a cease-fire in place for all Vietnamese troops. But it turned out that this was an offer for an unspecified future date; calling for an immediate cease-fire would have been giving in to North Vietnam's major demand, and Nixon was not ready to do this.

The American military was helping the Saigon army prepare for a major offensive against the Vietnamese communists' positions in Laos in February 1971. This proved to be a disaster. Even with massive U.S. air support, the South Vietnamese were forced to retreat.

Nixon's rating among the American people for the conduct of the war dropped to 34 percent. Even sections of the military were concluding that the futility and frustrations of the war, along with drug use, were ruining America's armed forces. Then in June 1971 the *New York Times* published the "Pentagon Papers," government documents including the secret studies carried out under Secretary of State McNamara that showed how and why the United States had gotten involved in the Vietnam War. The effect was electric. Many of the worst fears of protestors and dissidents were borne out by the enormous stack of papers, which documented everything from the cable describing U.S. involvement in the coup that overthrew Diem to the intelligence agencies' assessments, given to Johnson, of the true chances for success in the war effort. The opponents of the war in Vietnam believed that the Pentagon Papers proved their case.

On February 21, 1972, Nixon carried off one of the boldest moves in modern diplomatic history, aimed at ending the war in Vietnam and reshaping America's view of the world. On that day Nixon became the first American president to go to communist China. By visiting one of Vietnam's two principal patrons, the president hoped to frighten Hanoi with the prospect of an American-Chinese entente that could cut off full Chinese support for the war. Kissinger and Nixon believed that by establishing diplomatic relations with communist China, the United States would be in a better bargaining position with the Soviet Union, North Vietnam's other major patron. The president and his adviser envisaged a triangle composed of the United States, China, and the Soviet Union, in which the United States could manipulate the two competing communist giants to its own advantage.

Nixon's visit to China steered attention away from the Pentagon Papers and allowed the president to recover his momentum. But one month later the Vietnamese communists launched a conventional offensive against the American and South Vietnamese armies, which were not prepared for 120,000 soldiers descending from the north in waves supported by the Viet Cong guerrillas. The South Vietnamese commanders performed badly. Although some of their troops were brave, the army as a whole could not stand up to the assault. The gradual U.S. withdrawal had left only 6,000 American combat troops, and ARVN was more on its own than ever before. This time ARVN lost territory and was forced to abandon outlying posts captured by communists. Nixon was discovering what Johnson had learned earlier about the North Vietnamese. He had written in his diary, "The real problem is that the enemy is willing to sacrifice in order to win, while the South Vietnamese simply aren't willing to pay that much of a price in order to avoid losing."

Privately Kissinger had told both the Soviet leader, Leonid Brezhnev, and Le Duc Tho, his Vietnamese counterpart at the secret talks, that the United States was willing to allow North Vietnamese to remain in place in the south for a cease-fire but that any further fighting, like the offensive, would lead to serious repercussions against the north and damage to U.S.–Soviet relations. Once again, however, the North Vietnamese were stubborn, believing they could win an outright military victory, and they refused Kissinger's offer of a cease-fire.

Faced with the deterioration of the South Vietnamese army and the territory under its control, Nixon went back to bombing North Vietnam to pressure Hanoi for a "peace with honor." He vowed that "the bastards have never been bombed like they're going to be bombed this time."

On May 8, 1972, he announced the bombing and the mining of Hanoi's port, the harbor of Haiphong. But at the same time Nixon said that the United States would withdraw its remaining troops within four months of a cease-fire and after the release of all American prisoners of war. (Because the United States had not officially declared war against Vietnam, the enemy refused to give American prisoners (POWs) the rights required under international law.) Along with the recovery of the bodies of Americans killed in the war, the question of the POWs became one of the most painful, emotional issues of the negotiations. American POWs were routinely mistreated and beaten. Hanoi refused to apologize for this treatment and complained that the Saigon government, and some American soldiers, showed even less respect for the North Vietnamese they captured.

The bombing maneuver worked in the short run. The American air force pounded the north, dropping over 110,000 tons of bombs within one month, proving to the north that its offensives could not win so long as the American air force protected the Saigon regime. And on May 20 Nixon met with Brezhnev at a historic summit in Moscow. His grand strategy was in place: to pressure North Vietnam from all sides by invading the communists' sanctuaries in neighboring Cambodia and Laos and by traveling to the capitals of Hanoi's patrons to show that the United States was improving relations with the two countries whose supplies were crucial for North Vietnam's war. Neither China nor the Soviet Union condemned the United States for the bombing of the north, which continued and was moving closer to Hanoi.

Finally the North Vietnamese asked to meet with Kissinger that autumn. American presidential elections were to be held in November, and all opinion polls showed that Nixon would easily defeat his Democratic opponent, Senator George McGovern of South Dakota. The North Vietnamese could not hope for a new president and better terms; they would have to deal with Nixon. When Le Duc Tho met Kissinger in Paris on October 8, he offered a compromise that he described as similar to an offer the Americans had made earlier: the two sides could reach a military settlement and postpone a political settlement. This required the Americans to compromise by allowing the North Vietnamese troops to remain in the south at the time of a cease-fire while all U.S. troops withdrew. The North Vietnamese, for their part, would drop their long-held demand that Thieu be replaced by a new provisional government. Instead, a "National Council of Reconciliation" would design a future political settlement at an unspecified date, which Kissinger said would be at a "decent interval" after the U.S. withdrawal. In other words, the Americans would be allowed to withdraw with honor by leaving their South Vietnamese ally in place. But with North Vietnamese forces in the south, it was doubtful that the South Vietnamese regime would last long once the Americans departed.

The one remaining problem was to inform the South Vietnamese that this agreement had been worked out behind their backs. Kissinger himself went to Saigon to inform Thieu, expecting some unpleasantness but optimistic that the peace could be signed on October 31 as scheduled. But Thieu, accusing Kissinger of negotiating "over our heads," rejected the terms. Nixon cabled Hanoi of the problem and asked for a delay. But the North Vietnamese were fearful that the whole negotiation process had been a hoax to assure Nixon's reelection. Kissinger, meanwhile, told the White House press corps that "peace is at hand. We believe an agreement is in sight." On November 7, 1972, Nixon won with over 60 percent of the vote, and he and Kissinger began planning for more negotiations with the North Vietnamese.

On November 20 Kissinger met in Paris with Le Duc Tho. Both men had new demands. The United States now reversed itself and said the North Vietnamese had to withdraw from the south. The North Vietnamese were opposed to that demand and to the Americans' intention to dramatically increase aid to Saigon in preparation for its new role, standing alone against the communists. Le Duc Tho refused most of the American demands and added more new conditions. Nixon responded by returning to his strategy of bombing Hanoi into submission.

On December 18 the Christmas bombing began. For eleven days and nights, waves of B-52s struck Hanoi and Haiphong. The air defenses had improved around Hanoi, and by the fourth day the North Vietnamese had shot down forty-three American pilots. But the saturation bombing continued, to the world's horror. The United Nations condemned the bombing, and major American and European newspapers denounced it with especially harsh words. The *Los Angeles Times* said the bombing was "beyond all reason." The pope called for an immediate end to it. By the time the bombing was over, approximately 1,600 civilians had died in the raids. The United States had dropped 40,000 tons of bombs and had lost thirty-three servicemen when their aircraft were shot down; thirty-one airmen were captured.

Thieu was satisfied with this show of American resolve and believed that Nixon promised him that the United States would return to protect South Vietnam if the north violated any peace accords. He also understood that he had no choice, that the United States could not continue supporting the war. Henry Kissinger and Le Duc Tho returned to Paris, and on January 27, 1973, they initialed an agreement that was nearly identical to the one they had put together in October. The bombing did not force the north to accept new compromises but did convince the Saigon government that the United States had been tough on the north. Both Kissinger and Le Duc Tho were later awarded the Nobel Peace Prize. Le Duc Tho refused to accept it, saying there was still no peace in Vietnam.

The cost of Nixon's four-year-long war for "peace

with honor" was enormous. The number of South Vietnamese who died on the battlefield in that time was 107,504; the communists lost over half a million; and American deaths numbered 20,553. Moreover this "peace" was short-lived. In 1975, two years after the accords were signed, the South Vietnamese government lost the war to the north; the Khmer Rouge communists won the war in Cambodia, and the communists of Laos marched into Vientiane to take control over that country.

A Decent Interval

After the peace accords were signed in Paris, prisoners were exchanged by all sides. American newspapers were filled with photographs of POWs rushing to the open arms of their families, who had waited years for their return. On March 29, 1973, the last acknowledged American prisoners of war were released by Hanoi and the last U.S. combat troops flew out of Saigon. The return of the POWs was the one public display of emotion marking the war's end. There were no national parades, no national homecomings. No matter what Nixon said about "peace with honor," the soldiers returning from Vietnam were met with silence.

And as Le Duc Tho had said, there was still no peace in Vietnam — or in Cambodia or Laos. The Paris accords made no provisions for a peaceful settlement in either country where Nixon had widened the American war. Because of restriction on war activity in Laos mandated by the Paris peace accords, the U.S. bombers directed all their attention to Cambodia, where the Khmer Rouge insurgents attempted a final offensive to capture that country. From the signing of the Paris accords until August 15, 1973, when Congress ordered a halt to the American air campaign over Cambodia, U.S. jets dropped over 500,000 tons of bombs on that country, halting the Khmer Rouge advance but also forcing hundreds of thousands of peasants from their homes. The bombing, paradoxically, had a powerful psychological impact on the Khmer Rouge, who considered themselves thereafter to be the superheroes of the Indochina War for surviving the bombs.

In Vietnam both sides broke the Paris peace accords in short order. The first year, as the South Vietnamese army tried to recover control of the countryside, it took nearly 1,000 casualties every month but with little to show for it. The United States rushed billions of dollars of aid to help Saigon, but ARVN registered no great victories on the battlefield. By December 1974 General Van Tien Dung, the new commander of the North Vietnamese army, had prepared the final campaign to capture the south and Saigon. The one question was whether the United States would send back its air force against the North Vietnamese during the final offensive.

Earlier in the summer, President Nixon had been forced to resign following the scandal involving presidential coverups known as Watergate. Several of the measures Nixon had taken to advance his Vietnam and Cambodian war policies were included in the charges against him. The North Vietnamese gambled that the new president, Gerald R. Ford, would not want to reopen the wound of the Vietnam War at the moment when America was trying to recover from the upheaval of Nixon's resignation.

To test American resolve, the North Vietnamese

attacked the province of Phuoc Long. No American B-52s came to ARVN's aid. Thieu sent urgent messages pleading with Washington to back up Nixon's pledge to protect South Vietnam from an open assault. Even though the United States was no longer fighting the war, Americans maintained a strong presence in the south and continued to pay the costs of the war. In the first months of 1975 Thieu turned to U.S. Ambassador Graham Martin, who had the discouraging task of telling the South Vietnamese leader that Washington could not help out until June for budgetary reasons.

Meanwhile the North Vietnamese started their grinding offensive. A CIA analyst, Frank Snepp, warned Washington and Saigon of the impending campaign, but it made no difference. Thieu oversaw one of the most chaotic withdrawals in military history in the face of the North Vietnamese campaign. First to go were posts in the Central Highlands, which triggered the flight of half a million refugees, both military and civilian. In the northern provinces the communists shelled the army and then the columns of fleeing refugees. On March 25 the city of Hue was captured. Then Da Nang was taken, and the Americans began planning their own full withdrawal. In Saigon both Thieu and Martin refused to believe the end was in sight.

In the first week of April CIA analyst Snepp met with his "best agent inside the [North Vietnamese] Communist high command," who told him that the North Vietnamese were now planning to take Saigon in time for Ho Chi Minh's birthday on May 19. Under strong pressure from the United States, Thieu resigned on April 21. Snepp escorted him to the airport, where the crying former leader thanked the CIA analyst for all the United States had done. Then Thieu put his suitcases, which Snepp believed were filled with gold bars, on the plane and left for exile in London. Later Thieu would accuse the United States of betraying the south, of abandoning the noncommunists.

In neighboring Cambodia the Khmer Rouge communists launched their final offensive on New Year's Day, 1975, and by mid-April they were close enough to Phnom Penh, the capital, to trigger the evacuation of the small American community there. On April 17 the Khmer Rouge marched into Phnom Penh and started a revolution that would surprise the world with its ferocity and severity.

On April 29 the United States finally ordered the full evacuation of Americans from Vietnam. They had twenty-four hours to get themselves and their Vietnamese dependents out of Saigon by helicopters and onto waiting aircraft carriers. As Vietnamese and Americans rushed to the U.S. Embassy, the prearranged meeting place, the city was being shelled by the communists. "Half of Saigon was clamoring at the locked embassy gates," one eyewitness said. Photographers captured the last scene of the American experiment in Vietnam as the crowds swarmed toward the embassy roof and grabbed for the ropes dangling from the hovering helicopters. The picture of a helicopter over the embassy became the symbol of America's defeat in Vietnam.

The next day, April 30, 1975, the North Vietnamese marched into Saigon and took the surrender.

AFTERWORD

Pᴿᴇsɪᴅᴇɴᴛ Gᴇʀᴀʟᴅ R. Fᴏʀᴅ ᴛʀɪᴇᴅ to convince Americans to put aside any discussion of Vietnam, saying, "America can regain the sense of pride that existed before Vietnam. But it cannot be achieved by refighting a war that is finished as far as America is concerned."

Vietnam was America's longest war and its first defeat. More than 55,000 Americans were killed, and nearly 3,000 were initially listed as missing in action, or MIA.

In November 1982 Vietnam veterans gathered in Washington to dedicate a somber black granite memorial wall to the American military personnel who died in the Vietnam War. The highly polished wedge of rock seems almost buried in a field in front of the Lincoln Memorial. The only ornamentation is the engraved names of those who died. It has become the most popular memorial in the capital, something like a wailing wall where friends and family can trace the names of their loved ones, and tourists can stand in awe, as they do at graveyards of those fallen in battle.

In Vietnam Hanoi's victory was followed by another war and the complete failure of communism. The Khmer Rouge in Cambodia started what they considered the "ultimate revolution," forcing all the people into rural labor camps and killing off whole sections of the population. The Khmer Rouge massacres were genocide, murdering people because of their race, religion, or political beliefs. By 1977 the Khmer Rouge had turned Cambodia into a hellhole. Its leaders, looking for a scapegoat, blamed the Vietnamese communists, saying they had subverted the revolution. The Khmer Rouge then attacked Vietnamese civilians on their common border. In December 1978 the Vietnamese counterattacked and took control of Cambodia.

The world condemned Vietnam for its occupation of a neighboring country. A few countries, however, applauded Hanoi for evicting the murderous Khmer Rouge. At the same time, Vietnamese began fleeing their country to escape from the war with Cambodia, from the miserable economic conditions created by communism, and from the increasingly harsh restrictions on everyday life. Many of these refugees were called "boat people" because they took to the seas in any available small craft, in search of a new home. Hundreds of thousands left Vietnam this way, bringing with them tales of great hardship. The international community, led by the United States, enforced sanctions against the Vietnamese to force them to withdraw from Cambodia and improve the refugee situation.

Under communism, Vietnam became one of the poorest countries in Asia. But in 1986 Vietnam began reforming its economy; by 1991 it had made large strides toward creating a market economy and was becoming a part of the international community again. The regime, however, made only small improvements in granting greater political freedoms and human rights. The United States will be the last country to establish diplomatic relations with the government of Vietnam, long after other nations of the world have done so.

In 1989 most of the Vietnamese army left Cambodia, and in 1991 a peace agreement was signed for that country. The United States opened an embassy in Phnom Penh for the first time since 1975. According to American pledges, the United States and Vietnam could establish diplomatic relations by 1993 and the trade embargos lifted. Then the war will be over.

BIBLIOGRAPHY

Buttinger, Joseph. *Vietnam: A Dragon Embattled.* Volume 1: *From Colonialism to the Vietminh.* New York: Frederick A. Praeger, 1967.

Caputo, Philip. *A Rumor of War.* New York: Holt, Rinehart and Winston, 1977.

Caute, David. *The Year of the Barricades: A Journey Through 1968.* New York: Harper and Row, 1988.

Chesneaux, Jean. *The Vietnamese Nation.* Sydney, Australia: Current Books, 1966.

Coedes, Georges. *The Making of South East Asia.* Berkeley, Calif.: University of California Press, 1962.

Cortwright, David. *Soldiers in Revolt: The American Military Today.* Garden City, N.Y.: Anchor Press/Doubleday, 1975.

Edelman, Bernard, editor. *Dear America: Letters Home from Vietnam*. New York: Pocket Books, 1985.

———. *Last Reflections on a War*. Garden City, N.Y.: Doubleday, 1967.

Fall, Bernard. *Hell in a Very Small Place: The Siege of Dien Bien Phu*. Philadelphia: J. B. Lippincott, 1967.

FitzGerald, Frances. *Fire in the Lake: The Vietnamese and the Americans in Vietnam*.New York: Vintage Books, 1973.

Gitlin, Todd. *The Sixties: Years of Hope, Days of Rage*. New York: Bantam Books, 1987.

Greene, Graham. *The Quiet American*. New York: Viking, 1955.

Halberstam, David. *The Best and the Brightest*. New York: Random House, 1972.

Hammer, Ellen J. *A Death in November: America in Vietnam, 1963*. New York: E. P. Dutton, 1987.

Harrison, James Pinckney. *The Endless War: Fifty Years of Struggle in Vietnam*. New York: Free Press, 1982.

Henderickson, Paul. "Self-Inflicted Pain." *Washington Post Magazine*, June 12, 1988.

Herr, Michael. *Dispatches*. New York: Alfred A. Knopf, 1977.

Herring, George C. *America's Longest War: The United States and Vietnam 1950–1975*. New York: John Wiley and Sons, 1979.

Ho Chi Minh. *Prison Diary*. Hanoi: Foreign Languages Publishing House, 1966.

Isaacs, Arnold R. *Without Honor: Defeat in Vietnam and Cambodia*. Baltimore: Johns Hopkins University Press, 1983.

Johnson, Lyndon Baines. *The Vantage Point: Perspective of the Presidency 1963–1969*. New York: Holt, Rinehart and Winston, 1971.

Kahin, George M. *Intervention: How America Became Involved in Vietnam*. New York: Alfred A. Knopf, 1986.

Karnow, Stanley. *Vietnam: A History*. New York: Viking, 1983.

Lacouture, Jean. *Ho Chi Minh: A Political Biography*. New York: Vintage Books, 1968.

Littauer, Raphael, and Norman Uphoff, editors. *The Air War in Indochina*. Boston: Beacon Press, 1972.

Lowenfels, Walter, editor. *Where is Vietnam: American Poets Respond*. Garden City, N.Y.: Anchor Books, 1967.

Luce, Don, and John Sommer. *Vietnam: The Unheard Voices*. Ithaca, N.Y.: Cornell University Press, 1969.

Luu Trong Lu. "Goodbye Again My Son," *Vietnam Quarterly* no. 2, Spring 1976.

Maclear, Michael, and Peter Arnett. *The Ten Thousand Day War: Vietnam 1945–1975*.New York: St. Martin's Press, 1981.

Marr, David G. *Vietnamese Anticolonialism*. Berkeley, Calif.: University of California Press, 1971.

Mason, Robert. *Chickenhawk*. New York: Viking, 1983.

McAlister, John T., Jr., and Paul Mus. *The Vietnamese and Their Revolution*. New York: Harper and Row, 1970.

Miller, Merle. *Lyndon: An Oral Biography*. New York: G. P. Putnam's Sons, 1980.

Munson, Glenn, editor. *Letters from Vietnam*. New York: Parallax Publishing, 1966.

Neilands, J. B., G. H. Orians, E. W. Pfeiffer, Alje Vennema, and Arthur H. Westing. *Harvest of Death*. New York: Free Press, 1972.

Oberdorfer, Don. *Tet: The Story of a Battle and Its Historic Aftermath*. Garden City, N.Y.: Doubleday, 1971.

Porter, Gareth, editor. *Vietnam: The Definitive Documentation of Human Decisions* Volume 2. Stanfordville, N.Y.: E. M. Coleman Enterprises, 1979.

Raskin, Marcus G., and Bernard B. Fall, editors. *The Vietnam Reader: Articles and Documents on American Foreign Policy and the Viet-nam Crisis*. New York: Random House, 1965.

Rousset, Pierre. *Communisme et Nationalisme Vietnamien: le Vietnam Entre Deux Guerres Mondiales*. Paris: Editions Galilee, 1978.

Schell, Jonathan. *The Village of Ben Suc*. New York: Alfred A. Knopf, 1967.

Schlesinger, Arthur M., Jr. *Robert Kennedy and His Times*. Boston: Houghton Mifflin, 1978.

Shawcross, William. *Sideshow: Kissinger, Nixon and the Destruction of Cambodia*.New York: Simon & Schuster, 1979.

Sheehan, Neil, Hedrick Smith, E. W. Kenworthy, and Fox Butterfield. *The Pentagon Papers: The Report on the Top Secret Vietnam Study as Published by the New York Times*. New York: Bantam Books, 1971.

Summers, Harry G., Jr. *On Strategy: A Critical Analysis of the Vietnam War*. Novato, Calif.: Presidio Press, 1982.

Terry, Wallace. *Bloods: An Oral History of the Vietnam War by Black Veterans*. New York: Random House, 1984.

Tuchman, Barbara W. *The March of Folly*. London: Abacus, 1986.

Vo Nguyen Giap. *People's War Against U.S. Aeronaval War*. Hanoi: Foreign Language Publishing House, 1975.

Westmoreland, William C. *A Soldier Reports*. Garden City, N.Y.: Doubleday, 1976.

INDEX

About the Author

Elizabeth Becker is the author of *When the War Was Over*, which won a Robert F. Kennedy Awards citation. Becker covered Southeast Asia for *The Washington Post* and *Newsweek* in the 1970s. She is one of only two foreign journalists to report from Pol Pot's Cambodia, for which she received an Overseas Press Club citation in 1979. She has a degree in Asian Studies from the University of Washington and has studied at the Kendriya Hindi Sansthan in Agra, India. She lives in Washington, D.C.